Mike Baker
Studies by Jason Sniff

**From running and wandering
to following**

Mike Baker & Jason Sniff

ON PURPOSE
FROM RUNNING AND WANDERING TO FOLLOWING

iUniverse books may be ordered through booksellers or by contacting:

iUniverse
1663 Liberty Drive
Bloomington, IN 47403
www.iuniverse.com
844-349-9409

Cover Design: Karen Norris
Video Production Team: Shawn Prokes, Annie Brzezinski, Jason Sniff
Editing Team: Sandi Knapp, Sue Taulbee, Sharon Naylor
Biblical Research: Sam Strange

ISBN: 978-1-6632-2220-6 (sc)
ISBN: 978-1-6632-2221-3 (hc)
ISBN: 978-1-6632-2222-0 (e)

Library of Congress Control Number: 2021908709

Printed in the United States of America.

iUniverse rev. date: 05/17/2021

CONTENTS

WHO AM I?

HOW CAN I?

CAN YOU SEND SOMEONE ELSE?

CAN I GO IN PEACE?

INTRODUCTION

In a recent conversation with my friend and mentor, J.K. Jones, he used a phrase that struck a chord in my soul. "It seems as if that was *on purpose*," he remarked. Truthfully, I can't remember what we were talking about, but the phrase took me back to my childhood. I recall my mom using the same two words when I was a kid and she detected that my intentions were not completely innocent. She would accuse me, saying, "You did that *on purpose*" (and she was usually right). *On purpose.* These two words from a friend's conversation and a childhood memory had just collided with my prayers, planning, and preparation for this all-church study on the life of Moses. I wondered, "Could these two words be an appropriate description of the last forty years of Moses' life, and something that thousands of Christ-followers could aspire to?" If so, this study from Exodus 3 & 4 could appropriately be called **On Purpose.**

But these two words are only part of the Moses story because, like most of our stories, much of his life was not *on purpose.* In fact, it would seem that for the first two thirds of his life, Moses didn't live intentionally at all. His was a long journey that eventually took him to the mountain of God and the discovery of his God-given purpose. I think our lives often look like his. Like Moses, we often spend years running (from a past thing, or to the next thing) or wandering through life in survival mode with no real sense of direction. All the while, we are oblivious to the reality that God is doing a work *in* us so that he can do a work *through* us. Instead of running or wandering, he desires that we follow. To that end, I'm praying that you will join me in this study as we consider six important questions from the life of Moses that will lead us to live *on purpose.*

Where am I? Our study begins with an eighty-year-old Moses being lured into the presence of God by a mysterious burning bush. He had a very long history of running and wandering. First, he ran from Egypt after an impulsive and ill-fated attempt to bring justice to his blood relatives who were under the bondage of slavery. Then, he wandered through the desert, miles from his new-found home in Midian, as he led the flocks of his father-in-law. This week's study will encourage each of us to identify where we are in life right now. This requires us to look at our upbringing, our past, and our current situation in life. There are no *right* or *wrong* answers here; the goal is to determine where we are as we begin this study. This will give all of us a chance to reflect on our own stories and share them with one another.

Who are you, God? This week will focus on God meeting us where we are and making himself known to us. At the bush, and after God tells Moses he will be sent to Egypt, Moses asks God who he is. Moses knows that the Israelites he is asked to deliver will want to know who is giving him the authority to attempt this rescue after their 400 years of slavery. God answers by saying, "I AM". God is not being a smart aleck in this instance. He is simply describing himself by his proper name, which we translate as *Lord, Jehovah, or Yahweh*. His name literally means "to be" or "to exist." Here's the lesson: There is no way we can live life *on purpose* without knowing the one who holds all existence together. The good news is that through Jesus, God has met us where we are. So when we too ask, "Who are you God?" the answer is clear. He is the one who loves us so much that he became flesh to dwell among us, to give us purpose, and cause us to live authentically in his love.

Who am I? Once we begin to understand who God is through his son Jesus, and when we grasp how powerful and awesome he truly is, the Holy Spirit calls us to examine ourselves and consider our unworthiness in comparison. In this scripture, it is clear that God has a specific purpose for Moses (to deliver God's people from the slavery of Egypt), but there, standing on holy ground, Moses balks and reminds God of his situation. He is just an obscure shepherd, on the run from the law, with no authority or resources to accomplish the purpose God has set before him. It's a perfectly good question when he asks in Exodus 3:11, "Who am I that I should go to Pharaoh...?" It's an appropriate question for us to consider as well. Who are we that God should use us to accomplish his purpose in this world? During this week we will learn to embrace how God sees us—not as insignificant and unimportant—but rather as creations of his own made to do good works (Ephesians 2:10). Who we believe we are doesn't really matter; it's who God says that we are in Jesus that we must claim as our identity.

How can I? This question challenges both our perceived abilities and the shortcomings we know we have. It must have been incredibly daunting for Moses to consider the scope of what God was calling him to do in light of his weaknesses. He was assigned to be God's mouthpiece, and that was a problem. Moses was "not eloquent" and was "slow of speech and of tongue." Literally, he tells God in Hebrew, "I am thick tongued." Surely this would disqualify him for this great mission. But there are three reasons Moses can accomplish this call. First, God will be with him (Exodus 3:12). Second, he will work miraculous signs through Moses' shepherd's staff. And third, he will be with his mouth. Here, with Moses, (and later the apostle Paul) we learn that God is made powerful in our weakness and that he will accomplish his purposes in us and through us. We only need to be willing to be used by him.

Can you send someone else? At this point, God had answered Moses' questions, given him a clear call to action, and given him full assurance that he would perform miracles on his behalf. So you would think Moses' next question would be "When do I start?" Instead, he asks, "Can you please send someone else?" The Bible tells us "The anger of the Lord was kindled" (Ex. 4:14). Or, as we might say, this question ticks God off. We can't be sure why Moses still didn't want to go. Maybe he didn't want to give up the comfort and security of the life he had come to know. Maybe the job still seemed too big. Perhaps he was afraid, lacked confidence, or was just plain lazy. It might be all of the above. This week, we'll learn along with Moses that living *on purpose* for God can sometimes be overwhelming, but that God has a solution for the times we would rather he send someone else. God's surprising answer? "Yes, I will send someone else...with you." In this teaching, we will learn that just as God sent Moses' brother Aaron to help him live *on purpose*, he also sends us brothers and sisters to walk beside us as we follow God's call.

Can I go in peace? Finally, there is one more issue that was a barrier for Moses. He was employed by and beholden to his father-in-law Jethro. Ancient reverence for elders would not permit Moses to pack up and head to Egypt without receiving Jethro's blessing for what God had called him to do. Jethro's response was "Go in peace." This is another reason we need each other to live *on purpose*. We need affirmation, encouragement, and blessing from one another to follow Jesus faithfully. We will conclude our forty-day study by affirming and blessing each other as we reflect upon what we have learned through this study about God's purpose for each of our lives.

Are you ready? Are you tired of running? Do you feel like you are wandering? Let's try a different way together. Let's follow Jesus, knowing that only he can bring true meaning and direction to every step we take. Only in following him can we truly live *on purpose*.

DAY ONE

Where Am I?

"Now Moses was keeping the flock of his father-in-law, Jethro, the priest of Midian, and he led his flock to the west side of the wilderness and came to Horeb, the mountain of God." Exodus 3:1

You are here. You may not see a star, or a dot like on the old shopping mall directories, but you are here, nonetheless. In fact, *here* is the only place anyone can truly be. And *here* is where our study begins because before we follow, we need to acknowledge where we are. Just as finding your location on a directory or map will help you get to where you want to go, figuring out where you are spiritually will help you take your next steps with God. This simple yet profound idea is our starting place for living life *on purpose.* So, where are you? Let's consider three possible answers to this question.

YOU ARE HERE - LITERALLY

As we encounter Moses in Exodus, chapter three, he was literally "on the west side of the wilderness and came to Horeb, the mountain of God" (3:1). He was there because of his job. He was a shepherd, and he often journeyed far from his home for weeks at a time, watching, protecting, following, and leading his sheep to places where they could graze. It's quite likely that Moses had been here before in the forty years he tended his father-in-law's flocks. On the map, he had taken a journey of hundreds of miles from the land of Midian. He had traveled north and west around the eastern tip of the Red Sea, and south into the wilderness of Sinai. We call this wandering. Moses could not have anticipated that this place of wandering would be a holy place, the place where he would find his purpose. But God had decided that this was the *here* where Moses would learn God's plan and purpose for him. I believe it's the same for us.

Like our ancient brother Moses, we can locate ourselves literally on a map. I've poked fun at where I've been for the last twenty-five years, but I guess the joke is on me, because it looks like God's place for me in the foreseeable future is Central Illinois. I am literally *here*, even as I write, in Bloomington/Normal, Illinois. Where are you, literally? What's your location on the map? This can be as general as the country or state of your residence, or as specific as the neighborhood you live in, or the street you live on. More specifically, you are reading these words somewhere. Maybe you're sitting in your favorite chair, behind your desk, in front of the fireplace, on your patio or deck, or at the kitchen table.

Take a second and notice your surroundings. This is your *here*. Could it be your *here* is the holy place where God will meet you and call you to live *on purpose*? If an obscure desert mountain was the end of Moses' wandering, there is no reason to believe that God can't use the exact place you are now to renew your journey with him. As you think about that, let's consider another place we find ourselves.

YOU ARE HERE – LIFE EXPERIENCE

Moses was 80 years old when he met God on the mountain that day. But there is far more to the story of how he found himself there. In fact, for half of his life, Moses had been a totally different person. Scripture tells us that he was born to a family of poor Hebrew slaves, but had grown up as the adopted son of Pharaoh's daughter in the palaces of Egypt. His unique childhood was a combination of faith and knowledge of the God of Abraham and education and worship of the many gods of Egypt. He probably sympathized with the oppressed of his race yet enjoyed the finest luxuries the royal life would have provided. This mixed-message upbringing and the resulting internal conflict are why he found himself here at this desert mountain. Moses was on the run.

Day One

According to the Exodus 2:11ff, Moses was running from a past that all had forgotten, except for Moses and God. At age forty, he had defended a Hebrew brother by murdering an Egyptian task master. That murder put Moses on Pharaoh's most-wanted list. The Bible sums up the running this way, "Moses fled from Pharaoh and stayed in the land of Midian" (Exodus 3:15b). But that is a short summation of a long and lonely journey. Moses ran hundreds of miles, past the Red Sea, through the desert, and to a remote region called Midian. His exhaustion was evident as he sat by a well. He found himself—like all people on the run—hungry, thirsty, tired, and constantly looking over his shoulder.

Like Moses, we have all arrived at our current *here* as a result of our own unique stories. Maybe you're a teen-ager or young adult and your life's story is shorter. Or maybe you're middle-aged or retired and your book of life has lots of chapters. But we are all here as a result of every step we've taken in our past. So, what's your story? Where were you born? What was your family like? What are the joyful events of your life? Scholarship? Graduation? Baptism? Wedding? Kids? Grandkids? What are the painful parts of your story? Trauma? Handicap? Mental illness? Death of a loved one? Failures?

Our stories are always more than just events. Relationships have also been part of our story and have brought us *here*. Many of these relational experiences have been positive: nurturing parents, caring teachers, healthy friendships, and faithful spouses. But sadly, some of our relational experiences have left deep scars: divorce, abuse, infidelity, abandonment, and betrayal.

Beyond the situations that we had no control over, our stories also include the times that we messed up. Most of us have regrets from our past. We have hurt someone deeply with words or violent actions. We have been careless with other's emotions in unhealthy relationships. We have partied too much, given in to sensual passions, or lied to save our skin. We have been selfish, self-serving, or self-promoting. We have ignored those who loved us most to impress those who never did. We have looked down on or even hated others because of their race, their social position, or their economic status. Many of us are running from our past just as Moses fled from Egypt into the desert. What are you running from? As you think about that, let's consider our location through one more lens.

YOU ARE HERE SPIRITUALLY

More important than the mountain location or Moses' place in life is the presence of God. We really don't know what Moses' spiritual beliefs were when he approached the burning bush that day. He had a father-in-law who was "a priest of Midian;" a religious leader who would have held to a blend of belief systems. Moses had been raised, at least in his earliest years, by a father and mother of Hebrew faith, but we don't know if it had become his own faith. What we do know is that here on Mt. Horeb is where God met Moses. And here is where living *on purpose* always begins.

There is something far more important than where you find yourself geographically today. God is pursuing you, and for this reason, and this reason alone, I can confidently tell you that you can live *on purpose*. God met Moses at a burning bush, but he meets you and me on a cross outside of Jerusalem. Yes, it's true; you and I are here. But what Jesus did there on that cross makes what comes next possible for us. Because of his death, burial, and resurrection, we no longer have to wander aimlessly or run from our past. In following Jesus, our life matters. We have a purpose as we follow him. So, you are here. But don't stay here. Let's move as he leads.

DAY TWO

You are here, Hagar

"So she called the name of the Lord who spoke to her, 'You are a God of seeing,' for she said, 'Truly here I have seen him who looks after me.' Therefore the well was called Beer-lahai-roi; it lies between Kadesh and Bered." Genesis 16:13&14

Hagar was sitting by a spring in the desert. She was lonely, far from home, and unsure of her future. Ironically, one of the meanings of her name was "flight," and she found herself there because she was fleeing an abusive relationship. Her situation was the unfortunate result of two godly people who took things into their own hands and created a huge relational mess. In the process, they harmed this innocent single mom. We are introduced to Hagar in Genesis Chapter 16 as a member of Abraham's household and a maid servant to his wife, Sarai.

At this point, she is a girl, maybe as young as 13 years old. She is a foreigner from Egypt (*Hagar* may also mean "stranger"). She is also a slave, relegated to a life of servanthood. Why do these three things matter? Because it's important to know that she has absolutely no control over what is going to happen. She is simply the pawn in Sarai's desperate effort to have a son for her husband Abraham. Sarai encourages Abraham to sleep with Hagar so that Sarai can have a son through her. Don't even try to view this ancient cultural practice through a modern-day lens—just know that this idea was not of the Lord. Sarai should have had more faith in God's plan and promises. Abraham should have refused this proposition for so many godly reasons. But he didn't and Hagar was caught in the middle.

Time does not permit me to share all of the details of the story from Genesis 16, but I will summarize. Hagar got pregnant. Sarai was jealous. Sarai blamed Abraham. Abraham told Sarai to do as she pleased with her servant. Sarai treated Hagar badly. Hagar ran away. And that's how she ended up *here* at a spring of water in the middle of the desert. And *here* is where God met her.

It was likely that Hagar had heard of God and his covenant with Abraham many times. She was probably included in all of the worship services and sacrifices. But as an outsider, she probably had no real understanding that this *God of Abraham* was God to her, too. But he was, and that's why he met her where she was by sending an angel. In her place of desperation, Hagar thought no one cared. Now she learned that God did care, and that he a plan for her and for her son Ishmael. In that moment, she learned that God saw even a lowly, foreign, female servant.

This is why she called him *El Roi* or "God of seeing." Knowing that God saw and knew her changed her entire perspective. Notice that her situation didn't change at all. Yet she returned to her mistress at God's command. So how did this desert spring that represented desperation, fear, and escape become a place called *Beer lahai roi* (literally "well of the Living One who sees me")? Because here is where Hagar realized that God saw her, knew what she was going through, and shared that he had a plan for her life.

Many of us, like Hagar, are where we are in life because of wrongs done to us. Maybe a parent, a spouse, an authority figure, or a former boyfriend or girlfriend has hurt us in ways that have scarred us. Many of us find ourselves at the well of hopelessness because of circumstances and situations that are out of our control. Still others of us are at a place in our lives where we seem to have no options or direction for our future.

And here's where Hagar's title for God becomes ours. Jesus also sees you at the well of your desperation, fear, and fleeing. There is no desert place to hide from him. No matter where you are as you read these words, Jesus sees you and knows your name. And regardless of your circumstance or place in life, he is able to take a bad situation and turn it into a blessing. That is what Jesus does. He sees our despair and pain. He knows the wrongs we have done, and those done to us. He is able to repair and redeem the situations we find ourselves in because of these wrongs. We know this is true because the Living One who saw Hagar in her desperation also sees us in our sin and struggles, and he gave his life so that we might live.

DAY THREE

You are here, Israel

"And Jacob was left alone. And a man wrestled with him until the breaking of the day. When he saw that he did not prevail against Jacob, he touched his hip socket, and Jacob's hip was put out of joint as he wrestled with him. Then he said, 'Let me go for, for the day has broken.' But Jacob said, 'I will not let you go unless you bless me.' And he said to him, 'What is your name?' And he said, 'Jacob.' Then he said, 'Your name shall no longer be called Jacob, but Israel, for you have wrestled (ESV "striven") with God and with men and have prevailed.'" Genesis 32:24-28

Jacob was on the east side of the Jabbok River, and as the sun rose, he forded the river to join his family. He was noticeably changed. He had arrived at this point as a result of a lifetime of taking just about everything he (quite literally) could get his hands on. During the birth process, he actually grabbed his older brother's heel, which gave him the name Jacob, meaning "to supplant" (literally "heel grabber"). That was only the beginning. Eventually, through deceit, Jacob had stolen his brother's birthright and blessing. Then when his brother threatened to kill him, he fled to the land of his ancestry and spent 20 years swindling and being swindled by his father-in-law Laban.

Jacob's outward struggle with others, however, was only an expression of an ongoing inner wrestling with God. We don't know why, but instead of finding his place and purpose in the faith of his father and grandfather,

7

he seemed to challenge God at every turn. Even as he fled for his life from his brother, Esau, and after a heavenly vision, he told God that he would follow him IF he prospered him and brought him back safely (see Genesis 28). So for 20 years, we see God's blessing and providence in Jacob's life through his wives and twelve sons—even when he's not very spiritual. But we also see the pain that wrestling with God and others caused in his life. This brought Jacob to the ford of the Jabbok River on the eve of seeing his brother for the first time since Esau had threatened to kill him.

Honestly, we are all like Jacob. Even as Christ-followers, we are prone to look out for our own good and grab ahold of whatever makes us happy. We also tend to manipulate others in our family, at work, in school, among our friends, and in our neighborhoods in order to get what we want. And like Jacob, we even attempt to wrestle with God. We simultaneously seek his presence and blessing for our lives yet insist on doing things our way and telling him what's best for us. While we may never experience a physical wrestling match with God's representative (likely an angel in Jacob's case, although some commentators believe this "man" was the pre-incarnate Christ), we wrestle with him spiritually all the time.

What wrestling match are you currently having with God? You may be thinking, "I'm not wrestling with God. Are you crazy?" But truly, our prayers, which often express our own will even as we believe we are seeking his will, can only be called "wrestling with God in prayer." We can even see a picture of this through our Lord and Savior, Jesus, on the night of his crucifixion as he prayed, "My father, if it be possible, let this cup pass from me; nevertheless, not as I will, but as you will" (Matthew 26:39). Let's consider the wrestling questions from this story.

What am I wrestling with God about right now?

Jacob's internal struggle was that he had cheated, manipulated, stolen from, and lied to just about every person in his life. This left him afraid of the repercussions of his sins. Laban had chased him down and now Esau was just ahead. He wanted God to protect him and deal mercifully with him, even though he hadn't given such grace to others. He knew that he was part of God's plan through Abraham, but he didn't have God's perspective. He couldn't see how it was all going to work out, so he often took matters into his own hands. God had probably come to bless him and reassure him, but instead of waiting, Jacob tried to force a blessing by picking a fight.

Our prayer life often looks this same way. God's intention is to bless us, but instead of asking him for strength, we often tell him how he should bless us. Give me this job. Help my kid. Watch over my health. Bless my business. Get me an awesome spouse, boyfriend, girlfriend, etc. We're trying to pin God down so that he will do it our way. Remember, God knows and wants what is best for you and that is what he will do in every circumstance. Like Jacob, we may feel vulnerable as we face our own fears, but God is with us, and will bring us through. Spend some time today thinking about what issues you are currently wrestling through with God. Then consider this: How is God using this wrestling to change me?

This truly incredible scene from Scripture brought two changes to Jacob. As dawn broke, the angel (the "man" in verse 24, representing God) seemed to use his supernatural power to throw Jacob's hip out of its socket, but this didn't deter Jacob from keeping him in a headlock and demanding a blessing. So Jacob's opponent blessed him with a new name. He changed his name to Israel, which means "wrestle or strive with God." This name was a blessing because it was the name of God's covenant and presence with Jacob, now Israel, moving forward. This new name would also represent his descendants (the 12 tribes of Israel) and eventually the church as the Israel of God. The other change about Jacob was his lifelong and noticeable limp.

Whatever you are wrestling with God about right now, because of Jesus, the end will be a blessing. In fact, if you are a follower of Jesus, you are promised a new identity. You are actually a new creation being made into the image of Christ as you look forward to eternity with him. And you'll probably walk there with a limp. Being made into his image is not easy because we don't always cooperate with the Holy Spirit's work in us. Ultimately, the pain of wrestling with God will set us on the path of following him more closely, as Jacob did.

Then we too will be found crossing the next river into the future... blessed and walking with a limp.

DAY FOUR

You are here, Elijah

"There he came to a cave and lodged in it. And behold, the word of the Lord came to him, and he said to him, 'What are you doing here, Elijah?' He said, 'I have been very jealous for the Lord, the God of hosts. For the people of Israel have broken your covenant, thrown down your altars, and killed your prophets with the sword, and I, even I only, am left, and they seek my life, to take it away.'" (I Kings 19:9-10)

Elijah, you are here at Horeb, the mountain of God, and you are exhausted. If Elijah's location sounds familiar, it is the same mountain where Moses had encountered God about 800 years earlier. In fact, these two Old Testament men who represent the Law and the Prophets will later appear together on another mountain, at the transfiguration of Jesus, to confirm that he is the embodiment of all God's words (see Matthew 17:1-13). But at this moment, Elijah was simply a prophet for God who was alone, afraid, and on the run. He was so tired that he literally collapsed along the way and begged God to take his life (I Kings 19:4). Why was he so tired?

Elijah was tired spiritually because he had just defeated the evil Queen Jezebel and her Baal-worshiping prophets on Mt. Carmel in a god vs. God showdown. Elijah had challenged the prophets of Baal to call on their god for fire to burn the sacrifice, and then he called on the true God to send his fire. When Baal's fire failed and God's fire fell, the people proclaimed God as Lord and destroyed the 800 prophets of Baal. It was an overwhelming victory for the prophet Elijah, but as anyone who has ever done something great for God can tell you, it's exhausting.

Not only was Elijah spiritually tired, but he was physically running on empty as well. The Bible tells us that after he won the victory at Mt. Carmel, he was overcome with the power of God's Spirit and ran ahead of King Ahab to Jezreel. That distance is roughly the equivalent of running a marathon. Unfortunately, after arriving at Jezreel, Queen Jezebel was told what Elijah had done on Mt. Carmel and she threatened to kill him. So, he "…ran for his life and came to Beersheba…," (I Kings 19:3) and then went another day's journey into the wilderness where he collapsed. He had traveled 26 miles east and over 100 miles south, and even though he knew his purpose as a prophet was clear and that God had used him in the victory over Baal, he was done!

It is difficult to find or know your purpose when you are tired. And yet, most of us live our lives at a pace that leaves us physically, emotionally, and spiritually exhausted. Many of us are not running from something; we're just running. We actually have a phrase in our culture that describes this lifestyle of never slowing down. It's called 24/7 (some have even added 365). Life like this becomes an ever-increasing and unending parade of activities, work, leisure, relationships, events, and appointments. A 24/7 mentality is an obstacle to living life *on purpose*. What should we do?

REST TO RENEW OR FIND YOUR PURPOSE

First, we need to take an intentional step toward slowing down and disconnecting from our normal activities and patterns. Elijah left Samaria and headed south toward the mountain of God. He just needed to get away from it all to renew his purpose. What intentional steps can you take to slow down and disconnect? Try getting away to a quiet place in nature (maybe a lake, river, or woods) for a day. Try fasting from the internet, social media, or media in general (go ahead—it won't hurt you!). Something I find helpful is a regular calendar and schedule review that I do to eliminate some non-essential events from my calendar. These are just a few ideas to get you started. How can you disconnect today? Make sure you take this step. If an Old Testament prophet needed to get away to the mountain, we do too. Wherever our mountain of solitude is, we must go there to find our purpose. As a preacher once said, "It's impossible to hear the voice of God at Mach speed." When and where will you go for rest and renewal?

Once you have made time and room for God to speak, you must ask him to speak and then listen. Once Elijah got to the mountain, it was a still small wind that represented the voice of God to him. When is the last time you opened your Bible, sat quietly, went on a hike, or listened to some worship music, and asked God to speak to you? He still speaks, you know. Ask him to speak to you today by his Spirit that lives in you. Quiet your heart. Read a verse from the Bible. Think. Watch. Listen. Be patient. God is speaking all the time. What is he saying to you today?

Finally, invite someone else into your purpose. When God spoke to Elijah on the mountain, he instructed him to go and call Elisha to join him in his prophetic ministry. Loneliness in the God-following life is one of the greatest causes of spiritual exhaustion. God made sure Elijah never again felt that he was "the only one" by giving him a running mate in Elisha. Over and over again during this *on purpose* journey, we are going to be reminded in a variety of ways that our purpose will be found in community. As you spend some time asking God to speak to you, ask him to reveal another believer who shares like passions and purposes for him. Who is he laying on your heart today?

After forty days, Elijah left the mountain refreshed, renewed, encouraged, rested, and filled with purpose. Prayerfully, this forty-day study will renew us in the same way. But it won't happen unless we slow down, disconnect, find our mountain, and listen for God's voice. Let's begin today.

DAY FIVE

You are here, Ethiopian Eunuch

"...And there was an Ethiopian, a eunuch, a court official of Candace, queen of the Ethiopians, who was in charge of all her treasure. He had come to Jerusalem to worship and was returning, seated in his chariot, and he was reading the prophet Isaiah. Now the passage he was reading was this: 'Like a sheep he was led to the slaughter and like a lamb before it's shearers is silent, so he opens not his mouth. In his humiliation justice was denied him. Who can describe his generation? For his life was taken away from the earth.' And as they were going along the road they came to some water, and the eunuch said, 'See here is water! What prevents me from being baptized?'" (Acts 8:27&28, 32&33, 36)

Ethiopian Eunuch, you are here, and you are searching. According to Acts 8, this unnamed royal official found himself parked somewhere on the desert road between Jerusalem and Gaza. This road was probably one of three major highways in the First century— this one going down in elevation from the heights of Jerusalem and heading south and east to the Mediterranean Sea. Once there, the eunuch would have taken another road along the coast, through Egypt, and then continued south until he reached his home in Ethiopia. He still had hundreds of miles to go, but for some reason, he stopped his chariot to read something very important.

This is where Philip the evangelist found him. An angel had told him to travel this road, and he was directed by the Holy Spirit to join

13

this Ethiopian's chariot (see Acts 8:26+28-29). As Philip approached the chariot, he heard the man reading a scroll from the prophet Isaiah and asked the man if he understood what he was reading. When the eunuch replied that he did not, Philip explained the passage to him. This man was sincerely searching for God but did not expect God to be searching for him. Here on a lonely road in middle of nowhere, God changed this man's purpose from serving a queen to serving the King. Let's learn from him today.

GOD REVEALS HIS PURPOSE TO THOSE WHO ARE SEARCHING FOR HIM

Even though we don't know this man's name, we know a lot about him. He was a high ranking official, so he was important. He was well-educated because he was reading the Old Testament in a foreign language. We know that he was rich because he was riding in a chariot and had a copy of the Isaiah scroll. And yet, he was searching for something more. Though not Jewish by race, he was a worshiper of the Hebrew God. On his recent trip to Jerusalem, he had likely prayed, sacrificed, sung, and sought spiritual connection near the temple. (Note: As a foreigner and eunuch he would not have been able to go past the courtyard of the Gentiles.) Maybe he had purchased this copy of the prophet Isaiah's words in Jerusalem and didn't want to wait to get home to read it. He knew this was God's inspired word, but he just didn't understand what he was reading.

This is important for us to grasp today. God foretold a day, through his prophet Jeremiah, that people would seek him and find him when they seek with all their hearts (Jeremiah 29:13). You don't have to understand God fully to seek him and want to know his purpose for your life. Some of you who are reading this right now may have more questions than answers about God, faith, Jesus, and the church. You're in good company, but God is not hiding. He wants to reveal himself to you in profound ways if you seek him with all your heart. If this *on purpose* study is your search for God, keep reading, because he wants to reveal to you what he revealed to this man from Ethiopia.

GOD REVEALS HIS PURPOSE THROUGH JESUS

As with all Scripture, this passage from what we now call Isaiah 53:7+8, was ultimately fulfilled in Jesus. We're not told exactly what Philip said as he explained this passage—just that beginning here, he told the good news of Jesus. It probably went something like this: "This passage is about God giving his son, Jesus, to die on a cross for your sin because he loved you so much. But there's more. He didn't stay dead. We are witnesses to this incredible truth. Jesus rose again on the third day and by believing in him, you too can live eternally because he has conquered the grave." This is the good news the official had been searching for all his life. He had found his purpose in Jesus. He declared faith in Jesus and when he came to some water, he was compelled to be baptized as a sign of his death to self and being raised to new life.

If you are reading these words right now and have not yet trusted Jesus as your Lord and Savior, why not do what this man from Acts 8 did? He said, "See, here is water! What prevents me from being baptized?" (Acts 8:36). It's a good question. What's preventing you from taking a step of faith and being baptized in the name of Jesus? Let me encourage you to think and pray about this and follow up with your small group leader or a pastor.

Right here. Right now. Are you searching for God and his purpose for your life in Jesus Christ? My prayer is that you are, because I know that if you are searching for him, you will find him. It doesn't matter if you are parked on the side of the road in a first century chariot or sitting in your living room in the 21st century. May we all be like this Ethiopian Eunuch today—stopping to take time to search for God and discover his will for our lives.

DAY SIX

You are here, John the Baptist

"John bore witness about him, and cried out, 'This was he of whom I said, 'He who comes after me ranks before me, because he was before me.' So they said to him, 'Who are you? We need to give an answer to those who sent us. What do you say about yourself?' He said, 'I am the voice of one crying out in the wilderness, "Make straight the way of the Lord," as the prophet Isaiah said.'" John 1:15, 22&23

John the Baptist, you are here in the wilderness of Judea because of words spoken 700 years earlier. It was the prophet Isaiah who prophesied that someone would get the people of God ready for the Messiah by proclaiming his coming (Isaiah 40:3). The following verses (also quoted by Martin Luther King, Jr. in his famous "I have a dream" speech) went on to predict "Every valley shall be lifted up, and every mountain and hill be made low; the uneven ground shall become level and the rough places a plain. And the glory of the Lord shall be revealed" (Isaiah 40:4&5). This "glory of the Lord" to be revealed pointed to Jesus when he came to earth to save his people from their sins. But first, he would be announced. And the ministry of announcing the Christ's arrival would be a preaching ministry in the desert by a man we know as John the Baptist.

John was in the desert, which was a strange place for him to be. It was strange because he belonged to a priestly family: he was the son of Zechariah and Elizabeth (see Luke 1:5-25, 57-66). This means John was of the tribe of Levi, the tribe appointed by God to serve in the temple by leading the people in prayers, worship, and sacrifice. Technically, his ministry should have been located in Jerusalem when it was his priestly division's time to serve (see Chronicles 8:12-14 to learn how highly organized the priestly duties were from the time of King Solomon forward). But John's God-determined place was not in the city of David. His purpose was lived out in the Judaean wilderness on the east side of the Jordan river.

We are told that John "grew and became strong in spirit, and he was in the wilderness until the day of his public appearance to Israel" (Luke 1:80). It is believed by many that at an early age he lived with a strict religious Jewish sect known as the Essenes (the same group that lived in Qumran and to whom we are indebted for the Dead Sea scrolls). His passionate and fiery delivery against the corruption of the religious establishment in Jerusalem was certainly in alignment with the Essenes. So it is no surprise that when John began "proclaiming a baptism of repentance for the forgiveness of sins" (Luke 3:3), he called the religious leaders "snakes" and told them to repent.

Still, John's main message was not condemnation of the Pharisees and Sadducees. His purpose in life was to get the people ready. They were expecting "Elijah the prophet before the great and awesome day of the Lord…" (Malachi 4:5). Here John was, in the desert (dressed like Elijah, by the way), stirring up huge crowds and baptizing them as a sign of repentance for their sins. When asked if he was the Messiah, it was the perfect set up for him to say, "I am not the Christ, but there is one coming after me" (Mark 1:7). By the time Jesus came along, John had already begun a movement of people who were looking for the Messiah and who were tired of the old religious leaders who had abused God's laws of mercy and grace. John was a voice in the wilderness, and he prepared the way for Jesus.

FIND YOUR PLACE

Just like John the Baptist, each of us will find our purpose in life in our own unique location. This is the exciting part about discovering that where we find ourselves is not a throwaway location. It is the one where God has appointed each of us to live; it is part of our Lord's great design. Just as John's calling was perfectly and uniquely suited for the desert and not the temple in Jerusalem, our own life purposes are perfectly suited for the places we find ourselves every day. As a preacher, I have found my place behind a pulpit with a Bible, but there are thousands of venues where my message can never go. Classrooms, gyms, athletic fields, office spaces, homes, streets, work vehicles, family and friend gatherings—these are all unique locations where my sermons may never be heard. Look around. Where you are is not an accident. Your *here* is where God has placed you as the preacher, a word that means "proclaimer," "teller," "announcer of good news."

FIND YOUR VOICE

Once you have found your wilderness, then like John you have to find your voice. Even for the boldest among us, I wouldn't suggest John's voice. Walking down the halls of your high school or office wing shouting, "Repent for the kingdom of God is at hand," may be speaking the truth, but it won't be very effective in winning people to Jesus. This is important. How do you express your faith in Jesus Christ to the people around you? The only answer you may not give is "I don't." God has designed each of us to give our testimony or witness (remember our word *martureo* from the Greek?). Some witness through soft encouragement. Some write notes or cards. Some go to foreign lands. Others talk easily of their faith to their friends. Many invite others to church or into their small groups. More are simply there to listen and give perspective when those closest to them are hurting. It is through thousands of voices, expressed in a variety of ways, that most people hear the good news of Jesus. How do you express that good news?

Today, may we find our place and our voice so that we can prepare the way for others to know Jesus as Lord and Savior.

DAY SEVEN

Your Sin Is Here

"And Aaron shall lay both his hands on the head of the live goat and confess over it all the iniquities of the people of Israel and all their transgressions, all their sins. And he shall put them on the head of the goat and send it away into the wilderness by the hand of the man who is in readiness. The goat shall bear all their iniquities on itself to a remote area and he shall let the goat go free in the wilderness." Leviticus 16:21-23

Sins of the people, you are here, wandering around in the wilderness far from those who committed you. This is the image of the ceremonial removal of sin that took place annually on the holiest day of the Jewish calendar. It was called the Day of Atonement (in Hebrew, *Yom Kippur*). Each year, right after the High Priest had entered into the Holy of Holies with the blood of the sin offering, the forgiveness for sin was illustrated by a transferring of all of the people's offenses against God to a goat. Sin now had a new location. Instead of remaining on the heads of the guilty ones who had committed those sins, all the sins of the people had now been laid on a substitute to bear them and take them away. This is where we get the term *scapegoat*.

Younger generations may be confused because "the GOAT" now signifies something very different. In current vernacular, GOAT is an acronym for Greatest of all Time. In the ancient world, however, being "the goat" held a negative connotation. It came from this 3,500-year-old ceremony involving a scapegoat. In sports, scapegoats are the ones who take the blame for the loss even though it wasn't all their fault. In politics, it's the official who goes to jail for the wrongs or missteps of the administration. In marriage, it's the innocent spouse who gets blamed for breaking up the sacred union. In every walk of life, there are scapegoats--people who are blamed for things they are not guilty of. In the Old Testament, this was a literal goat who was blamed for the sins of the people of God.

Actually, there were two goats in this ceremony, and both of them are important as we begin this journey to discover life *on purpose*. The first goat helps us understand the price for sin. In our reading today, we have three words to describe how we disobey God. The word *iniquity* (Hebrew word *a von*) means "to bend or twist God's ways." The word *transgression* (Hebrew word *peh shah'*) means "to rebel against God's ways." And the word *sin* (Hebrew word *khat ta a'*) means "to miss the mark that God has designed for us." All of these, then and now, are in opposition to a perfect and holy God, and there is a price to be paid for them. On Yom Kippur, the price was the life of the first goat whose blood was then carried into the Most Holy Place as a symbol of atonement before God. The sin was covered by the blood.

In order to live *on purpose*, we have to consider our sin. No one comes to God as perfect. The Bible tells us, "For all have sinned and fall short of the glory of God" (Romans 3:23). Consider with me the times that you have twisted God's truth into something that agrees with the way you want to live. Consider the times you have intentionally rebelled against God when you knew something was wrong but did it anyway. And finally, how about those times you just missed God's will for your life?

How can we ever make up for all this sin? *We* can't, so a sacrifice must be made. The first goat is the image of Jesus atoning for our sins when he shed his blood on the cross. On the Day of Atonement, this sinless goat paid with his life for the sake of the people of Israel. "For our sake God made him (Jesus) to be sin who knew no sin, so that in him we might become the righteousness of God" (II Corinthians 5:21). This means we can have purpose for a righteous God because he has made us righteous through Jesus.

This brings us back to the second goat. What a scene it must have been as that goat was led to the High Priest (perhaps acting a bit skittish because of what had happened to the other goat) in the presence of all the people. Dramatically, the High Priest would place both hands on the head of the goat, as in blessing, but instead, he would confess the sins of the people. We're not sure of the details, but when the priest was done, the goat symbolically now carried the weight of the sin of millions of people. Then he was led into the wilderness, never to be seen again. Great care was taken to make sure the goat was led far, far away. You didn't want sin wandering back into town.

In order to live *on purpose*, we must consider how God took our sin away. This goat sent to the wilderness is a picture of that. Jesus didn't just *pay* for our sins--he *took them away*. I know many of us have considered our past during this week, and we may see our past sin as an obstacle to living *on purpose*. Well, I've got good news for you-- through Jesus, your sin is gone. Yes, that sin. That one too. You can remember them if you choose to, but God doesn't. He sent your sin out of the camp through Jesus' sacrificial death, and it's not coming back. He predicted this through the prophet Jeremiah and confirmed it through the writer of Hebrews, "For I will forgive their iniquity, and I will remember their sin no more" (Jeremiah 31:34 and Hebrews 8:12).

Life *on purpose* is possible because we don't bear our sin anymore. All of our sins, and our transgressions, and all of our iniquities—all of them—have been transferred to Jesus. He paid for them on the cross and took them away by his blood. He is the eternal scapegoat. He is the one blamed for our sin, even though he was sinless. And he *is* the GOAT, truly the Greatest Of All Time because only he could do what he has done for us. Consider this as we end our first week of *on purpose*. Where you are and where you are going is only possible because of where Jesus has gone.

ON PURPOSE: FROM RUNNING AND WANDERING TO FOLLOWING

Small Group Experience Introduction

Now more than ever how we live matters. The influence and impact of our decisions, choices, and behaviors have a profound effect on the world around us. As Christ followers, we are called to live every day on a mission that is critical to God's purposes. That sounds wonderful in theory, but for some our journey is confusing, exhausting, and void of clarity and meaning. It may be because of choices we've made; much of our life experience is due to circumstances beyond our control. As we evaluate all we face and know today, how can we live *on purpose*?

How can we "[D}o everything in the name of the Lord Jesus"? (Colossians 3:17). How can we focus our journey on what God is calling us to do? Your small group experience over the next six weeks will help you remember, understand, and practice specific concepts that will help you live with purpose. Here's how to navigate each week:

- **Listen to and remember the Sunday Sermons**: Each week starts on Sunday with our corporate worship gathering. Commit to attending online or in person. Take notes and ask the Holy Spirit to open your heart and mind to hear and understand the message.

- **Explore the Daily Readings:** Beginning with Sunday, each week has daily readings that guide you deeper into each week's theme.

- **Engage in the Small Group Experience:** Commit to engage in this study with others. Join an existing small group, start a new one, or simply invite a few friends to learn with you. There are a weekly teaching video and questions to help you understand and consider each week's ideas.

- **Apply everything:** In order to take your next steps with Jesus, it is important to decide how you will do this in your life. Each week has group or individual exercises to help you discover real ways to be purposeful.

In addition to the weekly group experience, there are resources available in the Appendix of this book. These will challenge you to go further and deeper into your *on purpose* life. The weekly teaching and leader videos can be found at www.eastviewresources.com.

One final thing. . . This study offers an opportunity for us to influence our families, neighbors, friends, and community. Now more than ever, you and I need to be intentional about following Jesus *on purpose* to help those around us do the same. We are called to live a life worthy of the Gospel (Philippians 1:27). With God's help and by following his calling, we can do this.

Are you ready?

Jason Sniff, On behalf of the entire Small Groups Team.

WHERE AM I?
EXODUS 3:1-6

Days 1-7

We each have a story. In fact, each of our stories is an epic journey and describes how we've lived our lives so far. As we reflect upon where we've been and where we are now, there are important questions to consider. Are we racing through life at a hurried pace? Are we wandering aimlessly through our days and weeks? What parts of our journey feels lost or unredeemable? How do we know what the next right thing to do is? Before we can determine what lies ahead, it's important to evaluate where we are. This week, we will take an honest snapshot of where we are in our life's journey.

First things first . . .

- If this is your first time gathering together as a small group, take a few minutes and allow members to introduce themselves (name, how long you've attended or known about Eastview, and what interests you about this study).

- If you've been together as a group for a while, have a few members share stories of a time when they were lost. What happened and how did each situation end?

Let's get started . . .

1. Recall a story of a time when you were lost. What happened and how did you get through it?

2. Let's review the Sunday sermon and the Day One reading. What main points and takeaways could you share?

3. Watch the "Where Am I?" teaching video and discuss the following questions:

    •   How does this teaching help you understand this week's idea?

    •   Where is your "Here?" Use two sentences or less to describe your "Here."

    •   What thoughts or questions do you have based upon the teaching?

4. Look back through this week's daily devotions. Which of the biblical characters did you identify with the most? What intrigued you the most or made you relate to that person?

5. What do you learn about Jesus from Day Seven's chapter on Leviticus 16? How does this explanation of God's required sacrifices affect how you are living your life? Are you making any sacrifices for God right now? Share your responses with one another.

6. As we journey through these next six weeks, we will take some time for a weekly group exercise to evaluate where we are in life and what next steps could help us define what it means to live on purpose.

    •   For this week, use page (#AppendixA Week 1.1#) to write out some reflections on your life's journey. Pay attention to where you've already been and where you are now in your journey with Jesus.

- As time permits, share this with your group. Be honest as you share. God is in every story and we can learn from one another.

Ok, so now what. . .

Final Takeaway. . . What is one way you will live on purpose this week?

_____

_____

_____

Next Steps. . .

- Apply your takeaway and live on purpose this week.

- Share your journey story with your family and a friend this week.

- Read the daily devotionals.

For Further Reflection. . .

- Complete the "Figure Out You're Here'" prompt that is located in the Appendix on page (##)

- Take the spiritual assessment located in the Appendix on page (#Appendiz A Week 1.2#)

DAY EIGHT

Who Are You, God?

"Then Moses said to God, 'If I come to the people of Israel and say to them, The God of your fathers has sent me to you,' and they ask me, 'What is his name? what shall I say to them?' God said to Moses, 'I AM WHO I AM.' And he said, 'Say this to the people of Israel; I AM has sent me to you. This is my name forever, and thus am I to be remembered throughout all generations.'"
Exodus 3:13-15

Several months ago, I got the conversation started in the small groups Sara and I are a part of (yes *groups*; we are in two) by asking everyone to share a nickname they had been given at some point in their lives. It was fun. Some were not surprising—like my friend whose last name is Shiflett becoming Shifty or my family name Baker being shortened to Bake. My wife was called Olive Oil growing up because she was skinny like that character in the old Popeye cartoons. Others were not so obvious. One of the young ladies in our group had the nickname Worm in high school which only made sense when she explained that she was a competitive softball player who was always in the dirt. Another guy in our group, who happens to be a cop, was nicknamed Hollywood because he always strikes a pose when there's a camera nearby.

Do you have a nickname? It is likely that you currently do or used to have an alternate name to the one your parents gave you. The term *nickname* comes from 14th century England where it was originally *eke* (a term for "another name"). Over the years it evolved into our word *nickname*, meaning a name that describes someone in fuller detail. Nicknames may describe our personality, our looks, our real name, or our phase of life. They are often given to us by relatives, coaches or friends, and sometimes they last a lifetime. And though these alternate names may sometimes be the only ones some know us by, they are not really our true names.

All of us were given real names by our parents when we were first born or adopted. And from the moment the nurse wrote it on our birth certificate, this name became the way each of us would be officially identified for the rest of our lives. Our full name (first, middle and last for most of us) is assigned a social security number, written or typed thousands of times on school assignments, and appears on our driver's license. This name is the one you'll respond to in conversation and what you will sign on official documents. But your name is more than just a legal designation.

People will know you mostly by your first name. They may identify your family by your last name and they probably won't know your middle name since it is usually relegated to an initial. But your first name will be the single most-used part of your identity, representing just who you are to those around you. Your name will be associated with your personality, your abilities, your physical appearance, and your life story. Go ahead and try this right now— just say someone's name aloud and notice that your mind is instantly flooded with everything about him or her. A name is important because it identifies that person.

If names are important in identifying each of us, how much more important is the name assigned to the creator of all the universe? This brings us back to the mountain and Moses' conversation with God. God has met Moses at the burning bush and has told him what he's about to do, but before Moses goes any further, he wants to know exactly who God is. As Moses considers the mission God is sending him on, he knows that the people God has sent him to deliver will question who is behind the directive and ask, "What is his name?" (Exodus 3:13). It's a good question.

At this point, the Hebrews had been enslaved in Egypt for over 400 years and although they knew the God of Abraham, Isaac and Jacob through their history and traditions, they were surrounded with hundreds of Egyptian gods. There was the sun god, the river god, the crocodile god, the god of harvest, and the god of war to name a few. Each of these *gods* had a different name. Maybe this is why Moses asks God to give him a specific name to represent him to his people in Egypt. But I think there is something more going on here.

I believe that the question Moses said the people might ask was really a question he himself wanted answered. As a Hebrew, Moses was certainly familiar with the true God of his fathers, but as grandson of Pharaoh, he was also well versed in the multi-theistic culture of the Egyptians. When mixed with the religion of his father-in-law Jethro (the priest of Midian, Ex. 18:1) who believed what was likely a mixture of folklore and Abraham's God, Moses was confused. So his question was sincere, "Who are you, God?"

Who you understand God to be is crucial to living *on purpose*. Maybe you're like Moses and have been exposed to a variety of gods, traditions, world views, and beliefs. Maybe you were raised in a faith other than Christianity. Maybe you don't believe in **G**od and have had no exposure to him at all. You may have been raised in the church and heard about God your whole life, but still you wonder who he is. And you may believe in the God of the Bible, but you are not sure that you really know him. So, we ask along with Moses, "Who are you, God?"

Well, God could have responded in many ways, because there are over one hundred names assigned to him in Scripture. We will examine some of these in future chapters. In the Bible, God is called *Creator, Provider, Healer, Lord of Armies, My Rock, Refuge,* and *Stronghold* just to mention a few. But to Moses, he gives the intimate and personal name that describes him in the strongest way. It is as if he is saying, "There are many names that describe me, but you can call me *I AM*."

This name in Hebrew is *ha ya* (like the sound we used to yell to Karate chop as kids) and it means literally "to be," " become," or "exist." What is God's answer to this all-important inquiry by Moses asking who he is? God's answer is "I exist." He goes on to say, "You can call me *I exist*" and adds, "This is my name forever, and thus I am to be remembered throughout all generations" (Exodus 3:15). The name that God goes by and the one that makes living *on purpose* possible is *I exist*. Why is it important to know this God of existing? Because if he is "existence," then all who exist can find their purpose only in him.

The best way for me to explain this all-encompassing nature of God as the great I AM, the one who is existence itself, is to reference an incredible

Jesus passage from Colossians. In Colossians 1:15-20, the apostle Paul is proclaiming that Jesus is God, and in doing so, gives us a clear explanation of what the name I AM truly expresses. There, he tells us that Jesus created all things. Everything was created by him. All the things "...in heaven and on earth, visible invisible... thrones... dominions... rulers... authorities" were made by Jesus (Colossians 1:16). He didn't just create these things; he created them for Himself. Jesus was before all these things. Jesus holds all these things together. Jesus is the beginning of all these things. He is the head of the church. Jesus is preeminent. Jesus has reconciled everything to Himself.

Who are you God? I AM is before creation, so he is bigger than my little world. I AM is the one who created everything, so he created me. I AM created everything for himself, so he created me for himself. I AM holds it all together, so he holds me together. I AM reconciled the world, so he can love and reconcile me. If all this is true, then knowing I AM is the only way my existence will ever make sense. Without him, life is only about running and wandering, but if he is who he says he is, then following him is the only way to live *on purpose*.

God knows who he is, but who is he to you? Remember, we are here. So, while we are here, let's answer this important question. Take some time this week and get to know God a little better. Write who God is to you personally on the blank page at the end of this section. This is your story of God and faith in him. Who is God to you?

DAY NINE

Who are you, God? ELOHIM

"Who are you, God?" ELOHIM. In the beginning, God created the heavens and the earth. The earth was without form and void, and darkness was over the face of the deep. And the Spirit of God was hovering over the face of the waters. And God said, 'Let the be light,' and there was light." (Genesis 1:1-3)

Before God formally introduced himself to Moses on the mountain and spoke his forever name, "The Lord," he was known more commonly as "God." This is the name Moses' ancestors knew him by and why he was called "The God of your fathers, the God of Abraham, the God of Isaac, and the God of Jacob" (Exodus 3:15). When 21st century Christ-followers hear or say the word *God*, we are referring to the one true ruler of the universe. But *God* is a word that was heard and understood differently by the ancient Hebrews. To them, the name was *Elohim*, and we can learn a lot from that name.

By the time the Children of Israel finally inherited the land that God had promised to Abraham, they had encountered a group of people who worshiped many different *els* (Hebrew word for god). A very popular *el* went by the name of *Baal* (see Numbers 25:3). Then there was an *el* named *Ashtoreth* who is mentioned in Judges 2:13. There was the *el, Chemosh,* (II Kings 23:13) and an *el* that went by the name *Molek* (Leviticus 20:2). These weren't the only gods worshiped in Canaan, but they were the most prominent. These gods are always spelled with a lower case "g" because

31

each is referred to simply as *el*, which is the generic Hebrew word for a "god" of any kind.

This is where God distinguishes himself from all other gods and why his name, Elohim, is always capitalized. Elohim is the plural form of the common word for God, *el*. Linguistically, this plural form of *el* communicates that he is greater than other gods. Literally, the name Elohim signified that he was the "god of all gods," "gods multiplied," or the "supreme god." Sometimes, *el* is used to form a compound name to describe God (as in *El Shaddai*, meaning "God Almighty"). However, no other god is ever referred to as Elohim. So who are you, God? "My name is Elohim—God above all gods—and everything you need to know about my name can be found in the opening verses of my story in Genesis."

I have said before (and this is not original with me) that if you believe everything in the first three verses of the Bible, the rest of the Bible will not be hard to understand. I would add that if you understand the God of these verses and what his name truly represents, you are on your way to knowing him and his purpose for you. He is God because there are no other "gods" or powers in the universe capable of doing all that is ascribed to him in the verses we have read today. Let's spend a few minutes in this passage, getting to know who Elohim is.

ELOHIM IS AN ETERNAL GOD

The story of humankind starts with "In the beginning" because this is the point where our history begins. And who is already there? Elohim. This means that he is eternally pre-existent to us and to this world. There has never been a time when God did not exist. This should humble us as we consider the implications of this reality. First, we are humbled as we understand that God is not dependent on us in any way. He was who he is before any of us ever came along. I like to say it this way, "God was fine without me." Second, the opposite is equally true; it is humbling to realize that we are dependent on God in every way. Since he made everything that we know and see, including our very lives, he holds the key to sustaining them all. Think of all the research that has been done to discover the vastness of the universe, the complexity of our DNA, the cures for human suffering, and the functions of the human brain. While we have made many discoveries and advances, only God truly understands all of these things because he made them. Third and finally, Elohim's position as pre-existent should humble us because since he chose to make us, he could just as easily choose to eliminate us.

ELOHIM HAS A CREATIVE AND POWERFUL WORD

We are told that God created the heavens and the earth, but it is his method of creation that amazes us. Nine times in chapter one of Genesis, we find the phrase, "And God said." This helps us understand the power of the word of God. The word for *said* is not just metaphorical in this phrase. It is the Hebrew word *a mar* which refers to the actual words that come out of one's mouth. Only the Trinity was there to hear it, but I believe God bellowed with power that reverberated throughout the universe, speaking his creative words over and over again: "Let there be light", "Let the waters gather", "Let the earth sprout", "Let the earth bring forth living creatures." What an incredible creation scene! Elohim spoke and everything that we see in our world came into existence in a spectacular exploding configuration.

ELOHIM IS LIGHT OVER DARKNESS

Finally, in these first verses of God's story, we learn that he has the power to overcome darkness (no matter how pervasive) with light. We are told that darkness was over the deep and in an instant that darkness was dispelled. On that first day of creation, God illustrated an eternal spiritual reality. No matter how dark it is, or how far that darkness extends, light will always overcome it. If you have ever struck a match in a dark room, or turned on your iPhone flashlight at night, or lit a candle during a power outage, you have experienced how even the smallest light dispels the deepest darkness.

There is so much more to understand about God in these verses as we are introduced to Elohim, but we'll stop here for now. Today, think and pray about how all of these truths about God were fully expressed in Jesus Christ, the living word of God. The apostle John begins his gospel account in a way that should sound familiar: "In the beginning was the Word, and the Word was with God, and the Word was God. He was in the beginning with God. All things were made through him, and without him was not anything made that was made. In him was life, and the life was the light of men. The light shines in the darkness, and the darkness has not overcome it" (John 1:1-5).

DAY TEN

Who are you, God? JEHOVAH JIREH

"And Abraham lifted up his eyes and looked, and behold, behind him was a ram, caught in a thicket by his horns. And Abraham went and took the ram and offered it up as a burnt offering instead of his son. So Abraham called the name of that place, 'The Lord will provide' as it is said to this day, "On the mount of the Lord it shall be provided" (Genesis 22:13&14).

It was a test all along, but Abraham didn't know it at the time. While Abraham was living in Ur of the Chaldees, God had said that he would make him the father of many nations if Abraham would trust him and go to the land of Canaan. God promised to bless Abraham with a son and then bless the whole world through his offspring. The problem was that Abraham was already 75 when God made the promise, and his wife, Sarah, had previously been unable to have children. But Abraham continued to trust God to provide a son who would eventually become a nation. God's promise was fulfilled twenty-five year later when God gave Abraham and Sarah a son who they named Isaac. That's why this test was so puzzling... and so hard. In Genesis 22:2, God said to Abraham, "Take your son, your only son Isaac, whom you love, and go to the land of Moriah, and offer him there as a burnt offering on one of the mountains of which I shall tell you" (Genesis 22:2). Who are you, God?

It is important to state here that unlike the "gods" of Canaan, God never required human sacrifice from his followers. We must remember this was a test. God was never going to let Abraham kill his son. His purpose was to increase Abraham's faith. If Abraham was willing to sacrifice the most important thing in his life, he would never again waiver in trusting God. Testing is how faith grows. None of us likes to be tested. But as we are, and as we continue to trust, we expand our faith. We discover what we really believe about who God is.

On this occasion, Abraham acted on what he truly believed about God. If you believe God, you will be obedient in every circumstance. Our ancient spiritual father inspires me because he took immediate steps to do what God told him: "So Abraham rose early in the morning, saddled his donkey, and took two of his young men with him, and his son Isaac. And he cut wood for the burnt offering and arose and went to the place God told him" (Genesis 22:3). When you trust that God will provide, you obey.

Notice the conversation between Abraham and his son as they ascended the mount for worship. Isaac had offered sacrifices with his dad before. They had brought the fire, and they were carrying the wood. But there was no animal to sacrifice. Here we see another statement about who Abraham believed God to be when he said, "God will provide for himself the lamb for a burnt offering, my son" (Genesis 22:8). When you trust God to provide, you don't need to know every detail of how something is going to turn out. You just trust that he has a plan.

In obedience, Abraham went through all the steps of a normal sacrifice until an angel stopped him and acknowledged Abraham's great faith in God, saying, "...[F]or now I know that you fear God" (Gen 22:12). And, as Abraham realized that he did not have to sacrifice his son, God revealed a ram caught in the thicket. God provided a sacrifice, just as Abraham believed he would. And Abraham and Isaac (who was greatly relieved, I'm sure) were able to worship God together with a sacrificial ram whose death and blood meant life for Isaac and a deepened faith for Abraham.

This episode caused Abraham to assign a new and descriptive name to God that helps us understand a little more about who he is. The name he blurted out was *"yehovah yireh"* or in its anglicized form, *Jehovah Jireh*. *Jehovah* is the name God told Moses on the mountain. It means "to exist" or "to be," and *Jireh* is the Hebrew word that means "to provide." Who are you, God? "I am the God who always provides." "I provide when it doesn't make sense and I provide in the most miraculous of ways." "I just want you to trust me, no matter what the situation is, to provide for you!" Abraham never forgot this place on the mountain where his faith was tested and where his God provided, a place called Jehovah Jireh.

If God were to test your faith today and he spoke to you audibly, what would he ask you to lay on the altar? What is your "only thing"? What is the thing you love most? What is the thing in your life that competes for your allegiance to God? God wants to know if you would be willing to sacrifice it. He is not asking you to do something flippant or irresponsible. He wants to know if you trust him. Every time that we are willing to kill something we idolize, we are stating by faith that God will provide, no matter what.

James says, "[T]he testing of your faith produces steadfastness..." (James 1:3). This is crucial for the *on purpose* life we're talking about because there will be times when our following doesn't make sense. We are no different than the men and women of faith in the Bible. We don't see the entirety of God's plan, nor do we always understand what he is doing in us. But because he is Jehovah Jireh, we know that he will provide all we need, all the time.

We believe this because there was another hill (some theologians think it was the same one), just outside of Jerusalem where a father took his son to sacrifice him. Only this time, an angel did not stop the taking of the son's life. Instead, the son died there because this was the plan and provision of the father. Just as the ram had taken the place of Isaac, Jesus has taken our place. God provided a way for us to live. Who are you, God? Jehovah Jireh.

DAY ELEVEN

Who are you, God? JEHOVAH RAPHE

"So Moses prayed for the people. And the Lord said to Moses, 'Make a fiery serpent and set it on a pole, and everyone who is bitten, when he sees it, shall live.' So Moses made a bronze serpent and set it on a pole. And if a serpent bit anyone, he would look at the bronze serpent and live" (Numbers 21:7c-9). "And as Moses lifted up the serpent in the wilderness, so must the Son of Man be lifted up, that whoever believes in him may have eternal life" (John 3:14). "And I, when I am lifted up from the earth will draw all people to myself." He said this to show by what kind of death he was going to die" (John 12:32).

It began where all pain and suffering begin, with our sin. After forty years of wandering in the desert, the people of God had still not learned to trust him in all circumstances. Now, as they moved up the east side of the Jordan and anticipated their entry into the Promised Land, they did the same thing they had done when they first came out of Egypt. They grumbled and complained about food and water. And so God sent fiery serpents as a punishment for their unbelief. We are told that many of them were bitten and some died. Witnessing that, it didn't take long for them to confess their sin to Moses and beg him to pray for God's healing.

The first time they had complained, the issue was also their hunger and thirst. Then they whined after finding a water source that was bitter and undrinkable. On that occasion, God miraculously healed the water so that they could drink it. Then he explained that just as he had healed the water, he would prevent any disease from coming upon them if they would only follow him. Then God revealed a little more about who he was by introducing himself as "...I am the Lord, your healer" (Exodus 15:27). In Hebrew, this is translated as *Jehovah Raphe* (pronounced Rah' fah).

Now back to the snakes. I don't know if you're like me and Indiana Jones, but I hate snakes! I cannot imagine the terror that spread throughout this complex campground as snakes slithered in and out of tents and went from one tent to another. I can imagine people running, parents panicking, startled students, and children screaming. In the midst of this chaos, Moses asked God to intervene and God gave Moses the weirdest of remedies. He told Moses to make a bronze snake, put it on a pole, and lift it up so that everyone who had been bitten could look up at the bronze snake and be healed. What! What?

Before we consider what God was up to in this ancient form of healing, I want to point out that a snake on a pole is still around 3,500 years later, and you've probably seen it at the place you go for healing. A snake wrapped around a pole is the symbol for most medical associations in the world, including the World Health Organization. This symbol has been attributed to Asclepius, the Greek God of healing. But I believe it may go back to the healing that Moses introduced in the wilderness and that the symbol was copied or adapted by Asclepius who came along almost a thousand years after Moses. That is just something extra to think about.

Back to the symbol itself. Why would God use the source of pain as a remedy to heal? I mean, if you've been bitten by a snake the last thing you want to do is look at a snake, especially a big bronze one on a pole. God is up to something here and is teaching us about how he expresses himself as Jehovah Raphe, the God who heals. Could it be that our healing God has the ability to turn the source of our pain into the source of our healing?

What is your pain right now? Is it physical? Do you have broken bones, a bad back, a serious illness, or chronic illness? Is your pain mental or emotional? Are you dealing with depression, insecurity, fear, or mental illness? Is your pain spiritual? Do you feel guilty, unworthy, trapped in sin, addicted, or lost? As I mentioned, our pain comes from sin--sins we have committed, sins committed against us, and the evil of this sin-sick world. Until we arrive on the other side of eternity, I don't think we will fully comprehend the complete devastation that sin has brought into our existence. Every pain we have can be attributed to sin, and the result of all this sin leads us to the greatest pain of all. According to Scripture, sin results in death. As Romans 6:23a tells us, "For the wages of sin are death."

This is where we see God's plan for the bronze snake on a pole. It was designed to be a picture of the greater healing that God had planned through Jesus' death on a cross. Since sin and death are the things that bring us the greatest pain, God brought healing by raising up death and sin on the cross of Jesus. Jehovah Raphe brought healing by offering his only Son Jesus to take away our sin and death by the shedding of his blood and his resurrection. There is no healing until we lift our eyes from our pain and look to the cross.

Whatever your fears are today, look to the cross. Whatever your pain is today, look to the cross. Whatever your sin is today, look to the cross. Whatever your insecurities and uncertainties are, look to the cross. And be healed by the God who heals.

DAY TWELVE

Who are you, God? JEHOVAH SABAOTH

"Then David said to the Philistine, 'You come to me with a sword and with a spear and with a javelin, but I come to you in the name of the Lord of hosts, the God of the armies of Israel, who you have defied. This day the Lord will deliver you into my hand, and I will strike you down and cut off your head. And I will give the dead bodies of the host of the Philistines this day to the birds of the air and to the wild beasts of the earth, that all may know that there is a God in Israel, and that all this assembly may know that the Lord saves not with sword and spear. For the battle is the Lord's, and he will give you into our hand'" (I Samuel 17:45-47).

When I was a boy growing up in the church, we sang a song about the famous battle scene from I Samuel 17 between David and Goliath. These lyrics, complete with hand motions that demonstrated spinning a sling above your head, are the way I learned the story:

Only a boy named David, only a little sling.
Only a boy named David, but he could pray and sing.
Only a boy named David, only a babbling brook.
Only a boy named David, but five little stones he took.
And one little stone went into the sling,
And the sling went round and round. (Repeat)
And round and round,

41

And round and round.
And round and round and round.
And one little stone went up in the air,
And the giant came tumbling down.

I grew up thinking that David won the day against the Philistines because he was such a good aim with his ancient slingshot. As kids, the natural conclusion from this song was that with God's help we too could slay a giant. And it wouldn't hurt to have some skill that God could use to his advantage, either. David's victory on this occasion is still used as an expression (especially in sports) for when the underdog beats the favorite: David beats Goliath. It's very exciting when the little guy wins. It was then, and it still is now. But, as it turns out, Goliath didn't die because David made a one-in-a-million shot to the forehead. Instead, Goliath fell that day because "The Lord of hosts, the God of the armies of Israel" fights for his people. Who are you God? I am the Lord (Jehovah) of hosts (Sabaoth: *tsa ba ote* in Hebrew).

In the Old Testament, the Hebrew word *tsaba* is used to describe the powerful and protecting force of an army. This word is used more than 450 times in the Jewish scriptures and is most commonly translated into the English word *army*. The word literally means, "that which goes forth" (as in an army going forth in battle). Occasionally, this word is used to indicate something other than large numbers of soldiers (e.g., "All the hosts of the heavens and earth" [Genesis 2:1] and angels as "hosts of heaven" [Psalm 148:2]). This was what the people of God in the Old Testament wanted and needed, a God who had the power and force of an army and would fight for them.

This raises the question for us: As Christ-followers, do we still need Jehovah Sabaoth? Most of us have never had an immediate need for an army. As students, we've never been challenged in the school cafeteria by a giant. We've never looked out of our front windows to find the house surrounded by invaders. Nor can any of us probably recall a time when we needed to have a weapon to defend our family or friends. It seems as if this name of God is no longer essential. If there is no battle, then the Lord of Armies is really not necessary. But there *is* a battle.

More formidable than any physical army you and I will ever face is the enemy who is trying to destroy us all. He is our enemy because he was first God's enemy. He was kicked out of heaven after starting a war against Michael, God's chief angel (see Revelation 12:7). Now that he has been banished to spiritual realms on earth, this "prince of this world," Satan, (John 12:31) is constantly attacking the human race. This is why Jesus prays "Protect them from the evil one" (John 17:15) and tells us to pray that we may be "delivered from the evil one" (Matthew 6:13; some manuscripts omit "one"). Peter calls him our enemy who "prowls around like a roaring lion" (I Peter 5:8) and Paul tells us that our battle is "against the cosmic powers over this present darkness, against the spiritual forces of evil in the heavenly places" (Ephesians 6:12).

So, should we go and find our slingshots and do some target practice? No. We need to remember that it wasn't a sword, spear, javelin, or even David's sling that won the battle 3,000 years ago. As it was then, it is now. It is only "in the name of the Lord of hosts" (Jehovah Sabaoth) that victory can be ours. As we look again at Ephesians 6, (verses 13-18) we find that God has given us every spiritual weapon of protection that we need. In the life of the believer, these are every bit as effective as David's sling. Remember that Jesus has already defeated Satan, so protect your mind with the helmet of salvation, guard your heart with the breastplate of righteousness, and when you feel that you are under attack, hold up the shield of faith to protect your soul. But our weapons are not just defensive. We can attack Satan's armies through prayer, with our feet in shoes always ready to share the gospel, and by holding it all together with the belt of truth.

Like David all those years ago--choose your weapon, but don't rely on it. And don't worry about the outcome—just get ready to watch giants fall. God's got this. After all, he is Jehovah Sabaoth.

DAY THIRTEEN

Who are you, God? My Stronghold

"I love you, O Lord, my strength. The Lord is my rock and my fortress and my deliverer, my God, my rock, in whom I take refuge, my shield, and the horn of my salvation, my stronghold. I call upon the Lord, who is worthy to be praised, and I am saved from my enemies"
(Psalm 18:1-3)

In modern day Israel, you can visit two ancient sites described in the verses above. By God's grace, I have visited both of them several times and I've been blessed to show others these incredible biblical places of refuge. Both were places to find safe haven from enemies, real or imagined, and both were retreat locations valued by two totally different kings. One was chiseled out of a stone mountain in the desert. The other still remains as one of nature's most beautiful, hidden oases. Ironically, these places are only separated by about 13 miles in the vicinity of the Dead Sea. The famous desert fortress is Masada and the other is a place called *En Gedi.*

Herod the Great was a friend of Caesar Augustus and was the official king of the Roman province of Judaea from approximately 37-4 BC. He was "great" because he was an incredible builder and was responsible for completing such architectural wonders as the seaport Caesarea, the Herodium, and the expansion of the Jewish temple in Jerusalem. However, behind this creative success was a paranoia that caused him to distrust and kill anyone he suspected was plotting to take his throne. This included many in his own family. His paranoia led him to build Masada.

In our scripture today, we actually find this word translated as *fortress* in verse two. But the Hebrew word that David wrote was *me tsa dah*, which means "the top of a mountain or rock." Though the fortress Herod built was not completed for another thousand years, David literally sang, "The Lord is…my Masada." David trusted God as his refuge, but Herod had no such faith. He built Masada as a place to run to and escape to in fear. This combination of palace and fortress was actually there before Herod, but he expanded it to include buildings, baths, storehouses, and soldiers' barracks for as many as a thousand men. Interestingly, there is no historical evidence that Herod ever actually went to Masada.

David was the Lord's anointed king, but he was constantly surrounded and pursued by enemies. In fact, during the first seven years of his reign, David's predecessor, King Saul, made multiple attempts to kill him. Though David was a great warrior and had 600 loyal men in his rag-tag, misfit militia, he was often outnumbered by Saul's army. When he was endangered, the place he repeatedly escaped to was a place called *En Gedi*, literally "spring of the goats." Here, as the name indicates, there was plenty of fresh water, and there were countless crags, cliffs, and mountains speckled with hundreds of caves.

While we can't be sure where David was when he wrote Psalm 18 (also recorded in II Samuel 22:2-4), he was probably thinking of En Gedi as he formed words of praise for his God. We are told in I Samuel 23:29, "David went up from there and lived in the strongholds of En Gedi." Here, the Hebrew word we introduced earlier, *me tsa dah,* is used. Both Herod and David had a *Masada* to run to for safety. But David's trust was not in the place but in his Lord. This is why David uses so many descriptive words that characterize a fortress to describe his God:

- The caves of En Gedi were a safe refuge because there, his enemies could not surprise him or overpower him. So it was for the Lord.

- The solid rock cliffs were not going to fall or crumble. So it was for David's God.

- The fortress that protected David and his men from arrows and spears reminded David how many times the Lord had protected him.

- When the horn of victory sounded and the enemies retreated, it was a victory that only God could bring.

- En Gedi was a place where David was saved, and there he was reminded that the Lord is a God who saves.

Who are you God? For David the answer was easy: "My stronghold." Do you have a place to flee to when you feel the enemy closing in? When life's circumstances lead to doubt, is there a solid place for you to stand? When you are afraid of the diagnosis, the finances, or the future, is there a safe place to go? When your mind is depressed, your soul is lonely, your heart is heavy, and your emotions are unreliable, do you know where to run? When you are being attacked by mean-spirited posts, ugly words, slanderous lies, or unfair criticisms, where do you seek solace?

Like Herod, you can try to withdraw and hide away in manmade solutions and trust in your own ability to overcome all that is against you. Or you can sing David's song that praises the Lord saying, "I am saved from my enemies." Know that *you* can sing this song too because the word for *saved* is the word *ya sha,* which is the root of the Hebrew name for Jesus (*ye' shua*). Jesus is a stronghold and whoever turns to him and away from our enemy, sin, will be saved. And this means we can run to him anytime. Where can you run today? To Jesus.

DAY FOURTEEN

Who are you, God? IMMANUEL

"Therefore the Lord himself will give you a sign. Behold the virgin shall conceive and bear a son and shall call his name Immanuel" (Isaiah 7:14). "She will bear a son, and you shall call his name Jesus, for he will save his people from their sins. All this took place to fulfill what the Lord had spoken by the prophet: 'Behold, the virgin shall conceive and bear a son, and they shall call his name Immanuel' (which means, God with us)" (Matthew 1:21-23).

On the final day of asking who God is, we come to one more name, and it may be the most remarkable one of all. Every name we have ascribed to God so far is beyond comprehension. God is the Lord, *Yahweh*, the very essence of existence. God is the creator of everything we see and know. God provides exactly what we need when we need it. God heals everything in our lives that brings us pain. God defends us with an army when we are under attack, and he is a safe place to hide when we are afraid. And all of these traits make this final explanation of who he is the most amazing name of all. This is the name that indicates that he *wants* to be with us.

The name is *Immanuel*. This name is a combination of two Hebrew words *eem* (with) and *el* (God). Seven hundred years before the birth of Christ, the prophet Isaiah used this name to foretell a time when God would actually be with us in the form of a son born to a virgin. This, of course, points to Jesus being born of the Virgin Mary as the angel declared to Joseph in Matthew 1. The prophecy fulfilled in Jesus at his birth is

47

celebrated every year at Christmas, but Immanuel is not just a name from a Christmas passage. I believe "God with us" is what God has always desired, and this is what the phrase "In the beginning..." from Genesis' 1:1 has gone to great lengths to accomplish. If we, like Moses, have been amazed at who God is on the mountain, we should be even more amazed that he desires to keep company with us.

God's original design was for mankind to be in fellowship with him. He made man (male and female) in his image so that we could relate to him, though never be equal to him. He wanted to create beings that he could love, share with, and enjoy companionship with. In love, he provided a garden paradise for his first created beings to live in. They enjoyed every sensory blessing--delicious and tasty foods, sunrises and sunsets, blue skies, sparking water, green plants, colored flowers in bloom, sexual attraction and pleasure, and a variety of birds and animals. It was truly amazing. But the most amazing thing is that God, our Elohim, Jehovah Jireh, Jehovah Rapha, Jehovah Sabaoth, and the Stronghold of David, wanted to be with Adam and Eve. When we find God "walking in the garden in the cool of the day" (Genesis 3:8), it seems to indicate that this was a normal daily experience. God, Adam, and Eve walking and talking together in the garden. God with man.

Unfortunately, sin broke their idyllic relationship. In disobeying God, man had shunned his presence. But God still wanted to be close to his creation. He spoke to them in dreams and appeared to them through angels and visions. He walked with a man named Enoch and made a covenant of peace with his great grandson, Noah. He promised the blessing of generations to a man named Abraham and through his grandson, Israel (Jacob), this family line fathered God's own nation. All of this showed his desire to get closer and closer to his creation, not just to be God as God, but as God *with them*. He was close, but he could get closer.

In the course of time, God would deliver these descendants of Jacob, now called Israel, from their bondage in Egypt so that they could be his people and he would be their God. He invited them to his mountain, Mt. Horeb, and revealed his presence through thunder, lightning and smoke. He was close, but he wanted to be closer.

On this mountain, God instructed Moses to build a tent in the midst of the Hebrew camp. It would be his dwelling place. So Moses built the tabernacle to the Lord's specifications and when it was completed, God's presence was visible to his people in a pillar of fire by night and a cloud by day. From the tabernacle, he was a neighbor to these people he loved, and he was close, but he could get closer.

After leading his people into the Promised Land and establishing them as a nation, it was time for God to have a permanent home. He chose the city of David, Jerusalem, as the place for his temple. So Solomon, David's son, built an incredible house where God's presence was represented in the most holy place. Through worship, sacrifice, and covenant, the people of God were close to the Lord, but God still wasn't close enough.

What more could he do? God had walked with his creation. He had talked with them and entered into covenants with them. He had delivered them, saved them, protected them, and led them. He camped with his people and lived in their main city. There was only one thing left. God BECAME man. The word that spoke creation into existence became flesh (John 1:14). The king of the universe took the form of a servant (Philippians 2:7). The Lord God of armies became obedient to death on a cross (Philippians 2:8). The healer healed us by his wounds for our transgressions (Isaiah 53:5). The Stronghold cried, "My God, My God, why have you forsaken me?" (Matthew 27:46).

He did all of this to be with us. Take some time today to consider who God is and why he wants to be with you. Must be love.

WHO ARE YOU, GOD?
EXODUS 3:7-22

Days 8-14

Ultimately none of us can live on purpose until we understand and know who Jesus really is. To know God is to know Jesus, so this week we will take an in-depth look at who God is, learn some of his names and see what they tell us about his character. During Moses's encounter with God, he needed to know who God really was. God answers Moses, but not in the way Moses expected. Living on purpose requires knowing that our God is "I Am," the name that will be remembered through all generations.

Let's get started . . .

1. Review your notes from Sunday's sermon and Day Eight's reading. What stood out and helped you come to a deeper understanding of God?

2. Watch the "Who Are You, God?" teaching video. Write down and discuss any key phrases or questions that surface from the teaching.

3. The daily devotional chapters focus on specific names of God that help us understand him more fully. Which name means the most to you personally and why? What is it about that name that encourages you or challenges you to live with more purpose?

4. How does knowing that Jesus is Immanuel, "God with us," change how you think about your daily habits and activities?

5. As a group, read together each Scripture passage from the daily devotionals. Notice the names of God as you read. As you hear each name of God, share what that name brings to mind.

6. If you haven't already done so, complete the journal prompt for this week found on **page (##)** and take some time to share your thoughts with the group.

7. As you end your time together, close with musical worship and prayer.

   • We recommend "O Praise the Name" (Anastasis)**(add you tube link and Spotify link)**

   • As you pray, take turns describing who God is. You may want to use the phrase, "God, you are . . . " and thank him for all that name means to you.

Ok, so now what . . .

Final Takeaway. . . What is one way you will live on purpose this week?
_____
_____
_____

Next Steps. . .

• Apply your takeaway.

• Keep reading the daily devotionals.

For Further Reflection. . .

- Study the passages located in the Appendix on **page (##)**

- Check out "I Am: Revealed" written by Mike Baker.

- Read and study *Knowledge of the Holy* by A.W. Tozer

DAY FIFTEEN

Who Am I?

"But Moses said to God, 'Who am I that I should go to Pharaoh and bring the children of Israel out of Egypt?' He said, 'But I will be with you...'" "Then Moses answered, 'But behold, they will not believe me or listen to my voice, for they will say, 'The Lord did not appear to you.' The Lord said to him, 'What is that in your hand?' He said, 'A staff.'" Exodus 3:10&11a, 4:1&2

Aside from being born on July 4, 1812, there was nothing special about John Jasper. He was not remarkable in his family, just one of twenty-four siblings. He didn't have any particular skills and spent his days on a tobacco farm removing the stems from cured leaves. He had no societal privilege or position because he'd been born into slavery near Richmond, Virginia. By his own admission, he wasn't a very spiritual man, having a propensity for womanizing and showing off. In his early years, there was nothing to indicate that God would use this man in a mighty way. But he did, and this young slave from Virginia grew up to become one of the most powerful and influential preachers in late eighteenth-century America.

While Jasper was still a young man, and still a slave, Jesus got ahold of his heart. Jasper asked a fellow slave to help him learn to read and write as he trained to become a Baptist minister. Even before the Civil War ended and he was given his freedom, he was gaining notoriety, mainly preaching at funerals for fellow slaves, but also preaching to Confederate soldiers. Soon, the newly freed Jasper founded the Sixth Mount Zion

Baptist Church in Richmond, Virginia. Within twenty years, his dynamic preaching and absolute belief in the infallibility of the Bible had caused his church to grow to over 2,500 people, attracting both blacks and whites! To the world, John Jasper may have been a nobody, but in God's hands he was one of the greatest preachers in American history. That's the way it is with God.

John Jasper admitted to the sin of his early years, but in the midst of that darkness, and even when God claimed his heart, he probably asked the universal question we all ask: "Who am I?" This is the question Moses asked when God met him on the mountain. The Lord had just revealed a God-sized purpose for the wandering shepherd's life when Moses asked this question. God announced that he was going to use Moses to free millions of slaves from the oppression of Egypt and then bring them into the Promised Land. God saw Moses as a part of his salvation story, but there was a problem. Moses didn't see himself the way God saw him. When the Lord looked at Moses, he saw great potential for him as a leader, but Moses saw an unworthy, unimportant, unknown shepherd with no credentials and no skills. His own view of who he was blurred Moses' vision of God's purpose for his life. Most of us feel the same way. "Who am I?" we ask with our ancient brother.

There are three *un* words that most of us are painfully aware of when it comes to discovering a God-sized purpose for our lives. They are *unworthy*, *unimportant*, and *unknown*. In spite of a culture that encourages supreme confidence in ourselves, I believe most people experience these feelings to varying degrees. Most of us simply don't see ourselves as qualified. Whether we feel inadequate because of teasing or bullying we went through in childhood, or because we never seemed to measure up to our parents' standards, or because we carry something from our past that we just cannot forget, we must deal with how we see ourselves before we can find God's purpose for our lives. Let's examine these three *un* words from the life of Moses and identify how they may have crept into our lives.

UNWORTHY

Moses may have asked "Who am I?" because he felt unworthy. At this point in Moses' life, he was a fugitive from Egypt. Forty years earlier he had fled a crime scene and the certain punishment of Pharaoh. As far as he knew, there were still Wanted posters there for his arrest. Moses must have thought, "God knows about my past. Who am I to speak for God when I am guilty of sinning against him? Who am I to lead a spiritual revolution when I'm a criminal?" From Moses' perspective, he was unworthy to be in the presence of God, let alone do something in his name.

Maybe you can relate. You may be thinking that this *on purpose* study is a waste of time for you because there is no way God could use someone with a past like yours. You may have committed adultery, belonged to a gang, sinned sexually, lied, stolen from a company, held racist views, abused others, failed your kids, been selfish, been addicted to drugs or alcohol, *etc.* Did I name something that made you wince because it hit too close to home? If nothing in the list above describes you, there may be some other reason you feel unworthy in the presence of God or his people. Consider this—If God only used people who were worthy, he wouldn't use anyone because no one is worthy before him. But he chooses and uses the unworthy because he's really good at taking imperfect, sinful people and giving them eternal purpose through his son, Jesus.

UNIMPORTANT

Moses may also have asked "Who am I?" because he saw himself as just a shepherd. After forty years of leading goats and sheep around the deserts of Midian and Sinai, he was probably pretty good at it. A good shepherd knows his animals and they know him. A good shepherd knows where to lead the flocks for water and green pastures. A good shepherd will lay down his life for the flock. But let's face it—this is not highly skilled labor. Anyone can learn how to do it. It is likely that his son Gershom was a shepherd as well. Like thousands of shepherds throughout these nomadic regions, Moses and his family lived a simple, humble, and boring life. "'Who am I to go to Pharaoh? I'm just a shepherd."

As you consider God's purpose for your life, how would you finish the sentence "I'm just a _____." I'm just a high schooler? I'm just a stay-at-home mom? I'm just a custodial worker? I'm just a retired teacher? I'm just in middle management? I'm just a youth coach? I'm just a call-center operator? All of these excuses (and many others) can be used to justify why we do not feel qualified to do anything for God. But this is where our view of ourselves and God's view of us varies wildly. He sees each and every one of us as important. Yes, you! It's true that God does see us as sheep, but we are important enough for him to send The Good Shepherd, Jesus, who knows us and leads us and chose to "lay down his life" for us (See John 10). You and I are important because God values us.

UNKNOWN

Finally, Moses may have asked "Who am I?" because he was a no-name man from Midian with no credentials that would cause the powerful Pharaoh to listen to him. Think about what God was calling Moses to do. He was supposed to approach the gold-and-jewel-adorned Pharaoh, in a throne room of great wealth and luxury, wearing a shepherd's robe and dusty sandals. He was to appear before a ruler who was worshiped as one of the Egyptian "gods" and whose words became law. But Moses was a shepherd with no power, authority, or title. How Pharaoh would scoff and laugh when this shepherd demanded the release of his entire Hebrew slave force. Picturing this scene is what Moses just could not imagine, and so he asked, "Who am I that I should go to Pharaoh?"

In much the same way, you and I may consider God's purpose for our lives and wonder how God could use a bunch of *nobodies* like us to make an eternal difference. But only when we realize that God has never created a *nobody* will we consider that he has a purpose for our existence. The scripture tells us, "if anyone is in Christ, he is a new creation" (II Corinthians 5:17) and that "we are [God's] workmanship, created in Christ Jesus for good works..." (Ephesians 2:10). If this is true, and I believe it is, God has a purpose for us regardless of how we see ourselves or how many times we ask, "Who am I?"

The great evangelist Dwight L. Moody was once quoted as saying, "Moses spent forty years thinking he was somebody; forty years discovering he was nobody; and forty discovering what God can do with a nobody." At this point on the mountain, Moses was still firmly in the nobody mindset. But he didn't feel that way at the end of his God-following journey because by then God had used him in a mighty way. I'm sure that most of us feel like Moses did on the mountain when God first told him that he was going to use him to deliver his people from the slavery of Egypt. But as we will see in the chapters that follow, God is really good at using so-called unworthy, unimportant, and unknown people to do amazing things in his name.

The turning point comes when God responds to Moses' question of self-worth. Look at the scripture again. God doesn't answer the question directly. God doesn't say "Moses, Moses, that murder thing is no big deal. It's been forty years; you've got to get over it." Or "This shepherd gig is holding you down. You are so much better than this." Or "Moses, no one knows you now, but they will. Someday you will be bigger than Pharaoh." In fact, God doesn't give Moses any kind of pep talk at all. He simply responds with "But I will be with you." And this is why Moses, and you and I, can live *on purpose.*

If we acknowledge reality, most of us are nobodies in the grand scheme of things. We all have a past filled with regrets and failures that make us feel unworthy. Most of us are just regular people, running, wandering, or stuck in our own lives with no title, name, or position worth mentioning. But who we are is not the most important part of the *on purpose* equation. Purpose is determined in Moses' life (and ours) by the God of the universe who tells us "I will be with you."

Could it be that while you are asking "Who am I?" God is answering "I will be with you" with a plan and purpose for your life? I am confident that this is true for every one of us who follows Jesus as Savior and Lord. We are worthy, important, and known to the only one who matters. How do I know this? I know it because the God who knows us, values us, and loves us, and sent his son for us. Who am I? The chosen one of God, whom he loves.

DAY SIXTEEN

Deborah: I'm just a woman

"Now Deborah, a prophetess, the wife of Lappidoth, was judging Israel at the time. She used to sit under the palm of Deborah between Ramah and Bethel in the hill country of Ephraim, and the people of Israel came up to her for judgment. Barak said to her, 'If you will go with me, I will go, but if you will not go with me, I will not go.' And she said to him, 'I will surely go with you. Nevertheless, the road on which you are going will not lead to your glory, for the Lord will sell Sisera into the hand of a woman.' Then Deborah arose and went with Barak to Kedesh." Judges 4:4&5, 8&9

Deborah was a woman in a man's world. I know that's a bit of a cliché', but if it ever was true, it was true in the days of the judges of Israel. In the time before they had a king, most of God's people were unfaithful to him, so this part of the history of Israel could be summed up in two contrasting phrases. The first is, "And the people of Israel did what was evil in the sight of the Lord" (Judges 2:11, 3:7, 3:12, etc...). And the second is, "Then the people of Israel cried out to the Lord, and the Lord raised up for them a deliverer" (Judges 3:9, 3:15, etc...). Since most of those whom God sent to oppress Israel were kings and their armies, the logical assumption would be that God would raise up a fighting man as a "deliverer" to challenge these enemies. And that's exactly what you find throughout this book of the Bible, except in the case of the judge, Deborah.

In all, there were eleven judges appointed by God, and Deborah (whose name means "bee") was the only woman to hold this title. When women in ministry ask me for a biblical role model, I always point them first to Deborah. There are many exemplary women in the Bible through whom God chose to accomplish his will, but in my opinion, Deborah ranks as one of the all-time greatest leaders in the Bible. There is also no doubt in my mind that in those days, just as now, there were men who didn't want to be led by a woman. In fact, we can also imagine that when God called her to be a judge, Deborah probably responded as Moses had before her: "**Who am I** to lead an army into battle or be a judge?" She may have thought, "This is a man's job." Yet God had called her.

Before we get to her role in the battle against the oppressive King Jabin, let's notice that Deborah had two distinct leadership qualities long before she found herself leading an army. First, she was a prophetess. In Hebrew, the female form of the word *nabi* was used for Deborah. This word signified one who received direct words from the Lord, and its root means "to bubble up". Properly understood, the Bible says that God gave Deborah words and she bubbled up those words and gave them to the people of God. She also used this spiritual ability in her second calling, which was as a judge. When we look at Judges 4, we find that there was a palm tree where Deborah sat and judged the cases of Israel. For forty years, she served and led Israel as a judge, but it was her victory over a Canaanite army and king that designated Deborah as "a mother in Israel" (Judges 5:7).

At some point during her tenure as a leader in Israel, her people were oppressed by a wicked king named Jabin and his equally sinister commander named Sisera. King Jabin's army was impressive (900 chariots) and continually oppressed Israel for twenty years. The people of God cried out, and God spoke to Deborah, instructing her to command Barak to call up an army to defeat these enemies of God. We don't know much about this warrior, Barak, who God chose, but he didn't seem as confident in his ability to fight Jabin's army as Deborah was. He told Deborah unequivocally that he wouldn't take Israel's army into battle unless she went with them. Deborah agreed, but then prophesied that Barak would not receive the glory for victory as most commanders did. Instead, the glory for defeating Israel's enemy would go to a woman. Then this judge and prophetess-turned-commander boldly led her people against Sisera, with Barak at her side.

One of the recurring *on purpose* themes we see in this section of our journey is clearly exhibited in the life of this Old Testament heroine whom God used in a powerful way. Here is that theme and truth: No matter who you think you are, it's who God thinks you are that really matters. Barak was called, through prophecy, to lead the army, but he didn't think he was capable of leading by himself. His response may have been, "I'm not a leader of God's armies." Deborah, on the other hand, had no military experience, but was able to fulfill this role because she knew her purpose in life. Deborah knew that it was God who made her a prophetess and judge and that she had never received a false word of prophecy or judgment from God. So she knew that if God's word was that his people's army would have victory over the enemy, she could ride confidently into battle.

Are you riding confidently into each day, ready to do what you have been called to do in God's name and trusting in his faithfulness? Are you the confident Deborah or the questioning Barak in this story? As we pray through and consider this question today, may God's Spirit begin to stir within us to clarify who he has created each of us to be in Christ Jesus. And may this lead to each of us to living life *on purpose* in the ways we see exemplified in the life of Deborah.

The end of the battle, the victory over the commander Sisera and his army, and the description of the glory going to a woman is all in Judges 4:17-22. Here, God shows us that when the people he has called follow him by faith, into his purposes, the victory is assured.

In this instance God used an unknown woman named Jael to drive his point home. LOL.

DAY SEVENTEEN

GIDEON: I am the least in my father's house.

"And the angel of the Lord appeared to him and said, 'The Lord is with you, O mighty man of valor.' And he said to him, 'Please, Lord, how can I save Israel? Behold, my clan is the weakest in Manasseh, and I am the least in my father's house.' And the Lord said to him, 'But I will be with you, and you shall strike the Midianites as one man.' Then the three companies blew the trumpets and broke the jars. They held in their left hands the torches, and in their right hands the trumpets to blow. And they cried out, 'A sword for the Lord and for Gideon!' Every man stood in his place around the camp, and all the army ran. They cried as they fled." (Judges 6:12, 14-16; 7:20&21)

Each time I read the story of Gideon I think of the childhood playground tradition of picking teams. Maybe kids don't still do this, but when I was growing up nearly every team sport started in this way. Kick ball, baseball, basketball, and even red-rover teams were formed by first selecting two captains (usually the oldest or best at everything). Then, everyone else would line up and the captains would alternate their picks of who they wanted on their teams. Finally, the process would end with the last unchosen kid standing there (head down) hearing the captain with the last pick reluctantly say, "Okay...I'll take you." I think Gideon felt like he was always that last one chosen, a left-over in the human equation that no one with any sense would ever choose for anything important. If you've ever felt like that last kid, keep reading because—surprise! God chose Gideon.

God chose Gideon as the man to deliver his people from the hand of the Midianites. There isn't space here to share every detail of his incredible story but let me encourage you to read it in its entirety (Judges, Chapters 6, 7, and 8). In the end, Gideon defeated God's enemies with an undersized army and unconventional weaponry, but that part of the story isn't our focus. Today, we will consider the questions Gideon had before the victory and how he processed them with God. From his example, we can learn how to work through our feelings of unworthiness using honest prayer. We can learn from Gideon as we continue to seek God's will for our own lives.

THE QUESTIONS

Gideon began by questioning why God had forsaken Israel (Judges 6:13) and why he had chosen him to defeat the enemy (Judges 6:15). Gideon knew just how formidable the Midian army was (135,000 strong according to Judges 8:10) and how small he was. I'm sure, the please in verse 15, was more like *puuuhleez*. How could a guy from a clan that Gideon describes as the weakest (the Hebrew word literally means "dangling," as in barely holding on) save anyone? Then he wanted to know how someone like himself ("least in my father's house") could make a difference. Often, when God calls us to something, we have these same questions.

Our questions for God often center on how small and helpless we feel and how big our challenges seem. Why did my wife get cancer? Why did my business fail? Why did I get cut from the team? Why was I born with physical or mental limitations? Why is there so much evil in the world? Why do bad people succeed? Why do children starve to death? I could go on and on. Do you have some God-sized *why* questions today? We learn from this story that God is not offended by our questions. When Gideon asked for several signs of reassurance, God honored his requests.

Let me encourage you to go to God today with your personal feelings of insignificance and with your questions about the overwhelming realities you are facing in your life. But don't just stop with questions. Ask God to show you his design for your life in clear and tangible ways. Yes, I *am* suggesting that we seek signs from God by "putting out fleeces" like

Gideon did in Judges 3:36-40. This may sound crazy, but if God was willing to confirm Gideon's call by making the ground dry and the lamb's fleece wet with dew, what makes us think he wouldn't respond to us in explicit ways? God doesn't tease us or confuse us. If we sincerely seek his direction and affirmation about what his calling is on our lives, I believe he will reveal it.

THE FLEECES

Over the years I've prayed this prayer many times: "God, if you make it obvious, I'll do it." Then I'll lay out a fleece—and this has taken many forms. If I get a scholarship to this school, I'll take that as a sign that you want me to go there. If a trusted Christian voice (my wife, my executive pastor, or my elder board) says "no," I'll move on. If a certain number of people show interest, I'll believe that is a ministry you want me to pursue. If a donor gives me a certain financial gift, that will affirm my call to the mission field. You can ask God to speak to you in any way you choose. Remember that this is not a game. Putting out a fleece is not asking God for a new car just because you want a new car. Your requests must reflect your sincere desire to seek God's will and direction for your life.

So what questions do you have about God's ability to use you? What ministry or calling feels far-fetched and overwhelming right now? Spend some time today thinking about a fleece, a question, that you could put before the Lord. Write it down. Then watch for God to answer. In today's scripture, when God called Gideon a mighty warrior, he wasn't talking about his military expertise or past successes. He only needed this "least in his family" to be "most in faith." In the end, Gideon *was* mighty in faith. And so it is for you and me. We see how small we are, but God sees what great things he can accomplish through us--if we will just trust him.

DAY EIGHTEEN

RUTH: I'm An Outsider

"But Ruth said, 'Do not urge me to leave you or to return from following you. For where you go, I will go, and where you lodge, I will lodge. Your people shall be my people, and your God my God. Where you die, I will die, and there will I be buried. May the Lord do so to me and more also if anything but death parts me from you.' And when Naomi saw a that she was determined to go with her, she said no more. So the two of them went on until they came to Bethlehem. And when they came to Bethlehem, the whole town was stirred because of them." (Ruth 1:16-19a)

You may have heard today's verses read during a wedding ceremony, and for good reason. These are some of the most eloquent and passionate words of devotion, faithfulness, and love in the entire Bible. They are uttered by the heroine of the book that bears her name. Ruth's words are not a romantic pledge to a male love interest (that would make this a Hallmark Channel movie). Instead, these are words spoken to her mother-in-law, Naomi, who had tried to convince Ruth to follow her sister-in-law and go "…back to her people and to her gods…" (Ruth 1:15). This seemed logical because Naomi was a descendant of Abraham and one of the covenant people of God, but Ruth was a Moabite. Yet Ruth made her choice to stay with Naomi and go to a land that was foreign to her. This leads to our consideration for today: Does God have a purpose for *outsiders* like Ruth?

Again, I'd like to encourage you to read Ruth's beautiful story in the four short chapters of the book of Ruth. But I'll summarize it for our purposes here. Naomi and Ruth were together because of a series of tragedies and hardships. Naomi and her husband Elimelech had gone to live in Moab because of a famine in their homeland. While they were there, Elimelech died, and Naomi's two sons married Moabite women. Then in the course of ten years, both sons also died, leaving Naomi and her daughters-in-law—all three of these women—as widows. No wonder Naomi changed her name to Mara (Ruth 1:20), which means "bitter." At this point, Naomi apparently heard from relatives in her hometown that the famine was over in Bethlehem. At this news, she resolved to return to her own people and encouraged her daughters-in-law to return to theirs. But Ruth refused to leave Naomi, even knowing that she would spend the rest of her life as an outsider.

Why was Ruth an outsider? Most significantly, she was a spiritual outsider to those living in Bethlehem because as a non-Jew, they would have thought of her as incapable of having a relationship with their God. She was also a young widow, which in their culture meant that her chance for remarriage was not good. And finally, there was the belief among the Old Testament people of God that the hardships that Ruth and Naomi had experienced reflected God's judgement upon them. The best Ruth could hope for was a meager existence, shared with Naomi, relying on ancient mercy laws designed to care for orphans and widows. How could God possibly have a purpose for someone who seemed so far from him, his mercy, and his people?

Before we answer that question, we should address those times when we feel like "God outsiders." There are many reasons that this can happen. Some people feel separated from God because of their pasts: "There is no way God could still love me after all I've done." Others feel far from God because they think they don't measure up: "I could never be as spiritual (or faithful, or smart, or devoted) as the people in the church." Many feel "left out" because they just didn't grow up in church or have never been to church. They think, "I just don't know how to act around Christians. If I ever went into a church, the roof would fall in." There are others who feel that they have nothing to offer: "I have nothing of value to offer God." All of these thoughts, and others, have caused many to feel like outsiders when it comes to God and his eternal purpose for them. Do you feel like an outsider? Have you ever? Now let's go back to Ruth's story.

In an incredible sequence of events, Ruth garnered the attention of a man named Boaz as she gleaned leftover grain in his fields during harvest. He gave his workers special instructions about her safety and even invited her to eat with him during a mid-day break. But it wasn't until Boaz sent extra grain home with Ruth as a gift for her mother-in-law that Naomi identified him as a near relative. And that is how Ruth was introduced to a custom of the people she had adopted. Here's how it is recorded for us in Ruth 3:9, "I am Ruth, your servant. Spread your wings over your servant, for you are a redeemer." Boaz did indeed redeem the whole situation by taking Ruth as his bride, which also redeemed Naomi's family name, her place in society, and her property. He paid the price to make Ruth an *insider*.

Before long, Ruth was with child and gave birth to a baby boy. And here's that word again. "Then the women said to Naomi, 'Blessed be the Lord, who has not left you this day without a redeemer...'" (Ruth 4:14). This is the lesson: For an outsider to become an insider, there has to be a redeemer. That's what Boaz was in this story, but his actions were only a picture of a bigger story. Jesus is the redeemer who bought us all with his death, burial, and resurrection. In him, there are no outsiders, because he has written everyone into his story. How do I know this? Well, the baby born to Ruth and Boaz in Bethlehem was named Obed, who was the grandpa of a more famous boy born in Bethlehem, whose name was David. He would eventually become God's king, but even he was only a picture of a distant future relative of his who would also be born in this little town where Ruth had been an outsider. I'm sure you've heard the story: "Unto you is born this day, in the city of David, a Savior who is Christ the Lord" (Luke 2:11).

Ruth, the Moabite. Ruth, the widow. Ruth, the one God had judged and cursed. Yet she became the great grandma of a king and an ancient ancestor of **THE** king. Ruth's name appears in only one other place in the Bible outside of these chapters. She is listed in the family tree of Jesus in Matthew 1:5. That's pretty good for an outsider. If God can take an outsider like Ruth and weave her into the story of salvation, he can do the same for you and me. All we need is a redeemer. That's who we have in Jesus.

DAY NINETEEN

TIMOTHY: I'm too young.

"Let no one despise you for your youth, but set the believers an example in speech, in conduct, in love, in faith, in purity." (I Timothy 4:12)

"The children now love luxury; they have bad manners, contempt for authority; they show disrespect for elders and love chatter in place of exercise. Children are now tyrants, not the servants of their households. They no longer rise when elders enter the room. They contradict their parents, chatter before company, gobble up dainties at the table, cross their legs, and tyrannize their teachers." I used to love sharing this quotation with parents and youth leaders when I was a youth pastor because when most people heard it, they assumed it was yet another diatribe about the current state of young people. In fact, though some historians now question it, this quotation is attributed to Socrates, circa 300 BC.

Obviously, it is easy to look down on younger people in any culture, in any era. I'm not sure why this is, but I believe it has something to do with getting old and grouchy and forgetting the days of our own youth. The truth is that younger generations have always seen things differently than older ones have, but that doesn't mean their viewpoints are always wrong. I've often pointed out that those of us in the older generation shouldn't complain too loudly about today's youth and young adults because we are the ones who raised them. I think that older Christ-followers should be the most patient and flexible people in the world as they set the example for the next generations of faith. We should pray for, encourage, nurture, and cheer on the young people in our church as Paul did when he wrote today's verses to his son in the faith, Timothy. But today's verses are not just a word of encouragement for youth--they are for us as well. Set an example.

For the younger readers of this chapter: You are really important to what God is doing in his church right now. You may not have wisdom, life experience, or a position of authority, and you may think, "I'm too young to have any real purpose in the church." Don't believe that lie for a minute because God has created you to have immense value, purpose, and position in the body of Christ, the church. Your generation will, in Jesus' name, bring positive change to the culture. Your generation will bring energy to the world-wide gospel message. Your generation will lead the "kingdom come" revolution in the church. Please don't let me or any other older Christian despise your youth. Don't be disrespectful or demanding, but live your life *on purpose* in our midst, and you will lead us. This is what Paul is saying to Timothy.

Timothy was a young church leader in a seemingly wise and experienced church setting. This meant that he struggled to be respected even though he was gifted and called to preach and teach the Word of God. His mentor, the apostle Paul, coached Timothy as he worked beside him and then through detailed letters (I Timothy 4:13&14, see also II Timothy 3:16-4:3). Yet there were some in the church who didn't approve of Timothy's youth and inexperience. What should he do? Paul didn't tell him to fight back, work harder, teach deeper lessons, or grow up; he simply told him to set an example.

The word translated *example* is the word *tupos* (as written by Paul in the First century). It literally means "to strike with a sharp object." It was commonly used to describe engraving or sculpting tools that were used to hammer stone, leaving a distinct mark. This is the word we get our English word *type* from. You type a letter on your keyboard, and it leaves a mark on the screen. Before computers, a manual *type*writer actually had metal keys which hit an inked ribbon and left a mark on the paper. Paul told Timothy that the key to leading others was not by demanding their respect and attention but by leaving a mark on them through how you conducted yourself. This is still true for young and old alike. The greatest way to influence others is to leave a mark—to set an example in the following five ways.

Leave a mark with your speech. What do your words tell others about who you are? Not long ago I was with some young Christian leaders, and it struck me that unless I had already known it, there was nothing in their language to indicate they were Christ-followers. I know we all want to be relevant, non-dogmatic, and able to speak the common language of the culture, but anyone can do that. If we want to leave a mark, our speech should be more gracious, less coarse, and should always point to Jesus. What mark are your words (spoken and posted) leaving today?

Leave a mark with your conduct. The greatest testimony we can give is the life that we live. People are watching us to see whether or not we are practicing what we preach. Our friends, family, and other acquaintances notice when we are kind, loving, and respectful toward others. The world is observing our work ethic, our honesty, and how we spend our money. If we want to mark those around us, we have to live out our faith—not perfectly—but sincerely. What mark are your actions leaving today?

Leave a mark with your love. The world talks about love. Every culture seeks love. Artists paint about love, and musicians sing about love. We all deeply desire to be loved. If this is true, then the greatest way that we can declare the love of Jesus to others is by loving as he loved. Jesus cared for those that others judged unworthy; so should we. Jesus' heart went out to the helpless and the hopeless; so should our hearts go out. Jesus brought healing to the unloved everywhere he went; so should we work to bring healing. Is the love you show others making a mark on their lives today?

Leave a mark with your faith. This is where young believers have an advantage over older Christians. And here is a confession from most of us over fifty: As we get older, we tend to protect ourselves more and more and take fewer of the risky steps of faith God may be calling us to take. In other words, we don't want to mess up or give up what we have. Just let us coast a little, please! But coasting is not what God calls us to do. I have found that younger Christians often have greater faith in an unseen future because they have little to lose. If you are young, seek God's grand vision for the church, believe in it and do it! Your faith will leave a mark.

Leave a mark with your purity. This is where the younger generation faces the greatest challenge. Their world is inundated with sexuality. It is on their phones and in their songs. Sexuality fills the movies and media. I believe it is harder than ever to stay pure, to preserve sex for its place in marriage as God designed it, and to submit to someone for accountability. Purity comes when you set boundaries for your technology and media intake and when you avoid situations where you may be tempted. It will not be easy, but when "everyone else" is buying into the world's lust, your abstinence from it will definitely leave a mark.

In the end, none of us can really control whether or not someone looks down on us, for our youth or some other reason. But we can set an example in these five areas. How are you leaving your mark today?

DAY TWENTY

"There was not a needy person among them, for as many as were owners of lands or houses sold them and brought the proceeds of what was sold and laid it at the apostles' feet, and it was distributed to each as any had need. Thus Joseph, who was also called Barnabas (which means son of encouragement), a Levite, a native of Cyprus, sold a field that belonged to him and brought the money and laid it at the apostles' feet." "While they were worshiping the Lord and fasting, the Holy Spirit said, 'Set apart for me Barnabas and Saul for the work to which I have called them.' Then after fasting and praying they laid their hands on them and sent them off." (Acts 4:34-37, 13:2-3).

In the early 1990's I worked for a ministry called *Christ In Youth* (CIY) whose primary purpose was to organize summer conferences to help students grow in their faith. CIY also offered short-term mission opportunities for qualified high school students. At the time, such international experiences were not as common as they are in many churches today. For that reason, there was a very detailed application process for any youth interested in participating. There were questionnaires to fill out, references to submit, and essays to be written before a student could be approved to go on these international missions. As I think of this months-long process, I wonder what Barnabas from the first Jerusalem church might have written in his mission application essay.

71

It's entirely possible that he never saw himself as a qualified missionary, but he was. In fact, he played an integral role in one of the greatest short-term mission trips of all time. Although "short term" in this case may have been for as long as two years, as is recorded for us in Acts 13 & 14. I would even suggest that Barnabas and Paul were the first to model the church as a sending agency for the gospel. The Antioch church that we read about in Acts 13 was a local church, sending and supporting people from their congregation to share the good news of Jesus into another part of the world. This is what churches have done for 2,000 years and what Eastview and numerous other churches continue to do. Barnabas was a ground breaker, a world changer, and a well-known leader in the early church, but he didn't start out that way.

When we first meet Barnabas, he was just one of thousands of members of the fledgling church that started on the Jewish holiday called Pentecost around 33 AD. There was no way he could have predicted that he would find his purpose for God as a missionary. He could easily have asked our question for this part of our study: "Who am I to be a missionary?" I think that many Christ-followers feel the same way, and this is why knowing Barnabas' story is important. This man dispels our preconceived notions about world missions. Barnabas shows us that you don't have to be a charismatic speaker, a radical revolutionary, or a great leader to live life *on purpose* and on mission. Why did the Holy Spirit call him by name to be a missionary? I believe there are clues in Barnabas' life, leading up to his calling, that made him uniquely qualified. I'm praying that his story will inspire our faith and prepare us for the mission God has for us. There are three attributes we can learn from Barnabas today.

GENEROSITY

The first thing we learn about Barnabas is that he was willing to give sacrificially for the cause of Christ and his church. This man, whose given name was Joseph, was a native of the island country of Cyprus (providentially the first stop on his mission trip). He was from the priestly tribe of Levi. He was part of the Jewish nation that had been dispersed (the *diaspora,* the scattering of the Jewish people in 70 AD after the fall of Jerusalem) worldwide but had come to Jerusalem for Pentecost where he experienced the miraculous beginning of the church. In fact, it seems that Barnabas was someone who invested early in the church. His donation is noted in Scripture and contrasted with the "gift" of Ananias and Sapphira early in Acts, chapter 6. The bottom line is that Barnabas' mission purpose was forged in generosity. Lesson: There is no way to have a mission mindset without being willing to give up worldly possessions.

ENCOURAGEMENT

The name Barnabas literally means "son of encouragement" and this is the name he was known by in the early church. What a great nickname! Imagine how empowering it must have been to be around a guy whose name meant "encouragement." Perhaps he gave courage (the meaning of the word *encouragement*) to apostles when they faced imprisonment, to widows when they faced injustice, and to the believers in the church when they faced criticism. Never underestimate the power of encouragement for those who are following Jesus. Barnabas helped others accomplish their calling because he encouraged them. Lesson: One of the most useful characteristics for living *on purpose* is the ability to encourage others in their mission.

LOYALTY

Barnabas was also loyal. He was one of the first people who believed and confirmed that Saul, once the church's persecutor, was now Paul, the fully converted church planter. He fearlessly vouched for him in the Jerusalem church, telling of Paul's Damascus Road experience and declaring him a true believer in the gospel of Jesus Christ (Acts 9:27). Later, when Barnabas saw the work that God was doing in the (mostly) Gentile church in Antioch, he personally went to find Paul in Tarsus and recruited him to the work in Antioch. This led to a year-long term of service, a team ministry in the church where Christ-followers were first called Christians (see Acts 11:22-26). It was during this time that the Holy Spirit called Barnabas and Paul to live their lives *on purpose.*

I need to say that Barnabas and Paul's experience is not a formula for being called or for finding your own purpose. There simply is no way to put God in a box. He chooses and calls us in his perfect knowledge, will, and purpose. However, when you develop the attributes exhibited by our ancient brother Barnabas, you are certain to find your calling. Are you generous? Are you an encourager? Are you loyal? Get ready. If you answered *yes* to any of these questions--get ready. You are close to God's call and purpose for your life.

DAY TWENTY-ONE

JESUS: I am

"Jesus answered, 'If I glorify myself, my glory is nothing. It is my Father who glorifies me, of whom you say, "He is our God." But you have not known him. I know him. If I were to say that I do not know him, I would be a liar like you, but I do know him and I keep his word. Your father Abraham rejoiced that he would see my day. He saw it and was glad.' So the Jews said to him, 'You are not yet fifty years old, and have you seen Abraham?' Jesus said to them, 'Before Abraham was, I am.' So they picked up stones to throw at him, but Jesus hid himself and went out of the temple." (John 8:54-59).

Wow. That escalated quickly. One moment Jesus was having a theological argument with the Jews about who he was, and the next moment they were ready to stone him. It's important to note here that "the Jews" were the Jewish leaders who represented the nation, not all of the Jewish people literally. But what was it that ticked off these dogmatic descendants of Abraham? Two words: *I am*. When Jesus said, "Before Abraham was, I am," he was intentionally referring to himself as the "I am" who introduced himself to Moses at the burning bush. In other words, Jesus was claiming to be God.

In fact, the book of John preserves for us seven "I am" statements that Jesus made during his ministry. Scholars believe that John recorded these sayings specifically so that Jesus' deity was confirmed to the gospel's original hearers. Truly, if the question we have considered this week had been posed to Jesus, his answer would have been clear. "Who am I? *I am.*" The first century leaders didn't believe he was God, but Jesus knew that he was. As his followers, we believe it too, so let's close this section of our *on purpose* journey and discover who we are by considering who Jesus is.

I AM THE BREAD OF LIFE (JOHN 6:35, 41, 48, 51)

The context of this statement was the miracle feeding of the 5,000, which Jesus accomplished with five loaves and two fish. Just as God sent bread from heaven for the children of Israel in the wilderness, Jesus miraculously created bread for his Jewish followers in the wilderness. These provisions were clear illustrations of Jesus as the bread of life. Only Jesus can satisfy the deep hunger of the human soul.

I AM THE LIGHT OF THE WORLD (JOHN 8:12)

Jesus made this statement as he taught on the southern steps of the temple complex in Jerusalem. The God who first spoke saying, "Let there be light" had come to light the way for those caught in a sin-darkened world. He was the "...light unto my path" and "...lamp unto my feet" (Psalm 119:105). Even now, in a culture that flounders in the darkness of sin, only Jesus can illuminate the way so that we can live in the light.

I AM THE DOOR OF THE SHEEP (JOHN 10:7&9)

One of the great metaphors of scripture is that of shepherd and sheep. As he described himself with this statement, Jesus gave us insight into ancient shepherding practices. After a day of grazing and leading his sheep, the shepherd looked for a place to bed down his flock for the night. Once he chose the location, the shepherd created a crude sheep pen of bramble, stones, bushes, or whatever he could find. He left only a small entrance for the sheep to pass through. When all the sheep had entered, he literally slept in the opening and became the door of the sheep pen. Jesus is the only entrance into the protection and safety of the shepherd's love and care.

I AM THE GOOD SHEPHERD (JOHN 10:11, 14)

Referring again to first century shepherding, Jesus declared that he was the good shepherd. We have many illustrations of shepherds as leaders in the Bible. Good leaders like King David shepherded the people of God well, and bad shepherds, like many Old Testament kings, neglected and abused God's flock. The defining mark of a good shepherd was that he cared more for the sheep than he did for his own life. A good shepherd would fight a mountain lion, a bear, or a wolf to defend his sheep. As the great shepherd, only Jesus could lay down his life for the sheep so that they could live forever.

I AM THE RESURRECTION AND THE LIFE (JOHN 11:25)

Jesus made this powerful statement in a conversation with his good friend Martha, whose brother Lazarus had just died. Jesus told her that her brother would rise again, and she confirmed that she knew he would rise in the resurrection on the last day. Jesus now revealed to Martha and her sister Mary that *he* was "the resurrection and the life." Then he went to Lazarus' tomb and gave them a glimpse into this spiritual reality: Only Jesus can resurrect and give life to someone who is dead, literally or spiritually.

I AM THE WAY, THE TRUTH, AND THE LIFE (JOHN 14:6)

As Jesus was preparing the disciples for his return to heaven after his resurrection, he told them that they would be reunited with him eternally in his father's house. When he assured them that they knew the way to where he was going, Thomas voiced their very real confusion, saying, "We don't know where you are going. How can we know the way?" (John 14:5). Jesus told them that they knew the way to God, the father—because they knew him. He said clearly, "I am the road to God." Jesus is the only way we can get to God.

I AM THE TRUE VINE (JOHN 15:1&5)

Finally, Jesus illustrated who he is from the world of viticulture (a fancy word for grape farming). His first century audience would have been well acquainted with vineyards and may even have snickered when he began his teaching. Jesus stated the obvious fact that when you cut a branch off of the vine, the branch withers and dies. Then he warned that if we are disconnected from him, we too will wither and die. Only Jesus can provide the spiritual nutrients that we need to bear fruit. Without a connection to him, we will die and be separated from him, the true vine.

As you finish this week of reflecting on who you are, reflect on Jesus, the "I am." The answer to "Who am I?" will not make sense unless you know who he is.

WHO AM I?
EXODUS 3:11, 4:1-9

Days 15 - 21

Once we begin to know who God really is, we can begin to understand who we are as his followers. You might be wondering, "What do I even have to offer?" This week we will learn that although we are unworthy, God accomplishes his purpose for us through the Holy Spirit's indwelling of believers, and his willingness to work within us. Our truest identity is only found in Jesus. Living on purpose shifts the question from a cynical "How could God possibly use me" to a spirit filled "How does God *want* to use me?"

Let's get started. . .

1. What stands out from Sunday's sermon and Day Fifteen devotional chapter that helps increase your understanding of who you are in God?

2. Watch this week's teaching video "Who Am I?" and jot down any phrases or questions you have about what is shared.

   • Knowing that your group is a safe environment, which of these three "un" words--unworthy, unimportant, unknown— do you sometimes use as an excuse not to seek God's purpose in your life?

   • Honestly answer the following phrase, "I am just a . . . ."

3. Which of the five people (Deborah, Gideon, Ruth, Timothy, or Barnabas) highlighted in this week's daily devotions has a journey that most resembles yours and why?

   • What did you learn about that person that could help you live your life on purpose?

4. Jesus' "I AM" statements highlighted in Day Twenty-one's chapter are not just declarations of his character. Each of them is a promise that can begin to heal our insecurities. Take some time to review those statements in John and identify which ones are most helpful to you right now.

5. As a group, refer to the "Who I AM in Christ" list found on page (#Appendix A 3.1#). These are statements of truth about who you and I are in Jesus.

   • Go around the circle and read them out loud.

   • Then choose and circle two or more truths that you will speak to yourself and to others every day this week.

6. Spend some time praying over one another in your group. If you have been together for some time, you may want to name specific encouraging truths you recognize in one another.

Ok, so now what. . .

Final Takeaway. . . What is one way you will live on purpose this week?

_____

_____

_____

Next Steps. . .

- Don't forget to speak these truths daily.

- If you haven't already, finish the writing prompt from Day Fifteen.

- Keep Reading and Take the Spiritual Gifts Assessment before your week 4 group gathering. *www.eastview.church/mygifts*

For Further Reflection. . .

- Part of God's purpose-filled plan is to use our weaknesses for His glory. Check out Appendix A 3.2 for further examples of people in the Bible and how God showed them their purpose and used them to further his kingdom.

DAY TWENTY-TWO

How Can I?

"But Moses said to the Lord, 'Oh, my Lord, I am not eloquent, either in the past nor since you have spoken to your servant, but I am slow of speech and of tongue.' Then the Lord said to him, 'Who has made man's mouth? Who makes him mute, or deaf, or seeing, or blind? Is it not I, the Lord? Now therefore go, and I will be with your mouth and teach you what you shall speak.'" Exodus 4:10-12

If you are like me, you are well aware of the things you can't do. I was thinking about those things as I read today's verses. Like Moses, I have a long of list things I'm not good at. To finish his sentence "Oh, my Lord, I am not.... " Oh, my Lord, I am not artistic. I can't even draw stick figures most of the time. Oh, my Lord, I am not able to focus. I have never been officially diagnosed with Attention Deficit Disorder, but just ask anyone who knows me. And like the late night TV sales pitch says, "But wait… that's not all."

I'm not good at technology, which can be frustrating in the tech-centric times we live in. I don't know how to work on a car. I am not mechanically inclined enough to work on an engine; there are too many parts to assemble and reassemble and too many steps for these clumsy hands. Similarly, I am not very good at building things. Some of my worst life experiences have been helping my wife put together furniture that she bought online. Honestly, I own about five tools.

My list continues. I could never figure out story problems in math class. I'd get lost somewhere between a train traveling south at five miles an hour passing a train going north. "But hey, who's on that train?" I would wonder. (See my self-diagnosed ADD comments above.) I am also a total failure when it comes to playing a musical instrument. I took guitar lessons for about three months early in my youth ministry career. All I can say is that it was a waste of time for my instructor. I could go on for days because the list of the things I can't do is endless. I'll bet you have a list of your own.

How would you finish the sentence that Moses cried out to the Lord? "Oh, my Lord, I am not….". What are the things you are not good at or simply can't do? As you think about your list, let's look more closely at Moses' story and learn what God thinks about the things we can't do.

As we read in today's verse, Moses has serious reservations about carrying out the new purpose God had revealed for him. He understands that God is asking him to be his spokesperson to the Israelites in slavery in Egypt and to the powerful Pharaoh there. The words that come from Moses' mouth will need to be not only persuasive and authoritative in the courts of Egypt's king but also inspirational and influential to the Hebrew people. As a preacher, I can tell you that fulfilling such widely varied needs is difficult even on my best speaking days. This is why Moses thought to himself, "How can I do this?"

So he reminds God of his inabilities. "Oh Lord, I am not eloquent… but I am slow of speech and tongue" (Exodus 4:10). We are not sure what Moses' speaking challenge was, but the Hebrew translation gives us a little insight. When Moses says he is "not eloquent" he is literally saying he is not *ish debarim* or not "a man of words." This doesn't help us know his issue specifically, because it could just be that he is an introvert. And maybe that was it; being a shepherd was a good lifestyle for an introvert. But there seems to be something else in the phrase "slow of speech and tongue." The more literal translation would be that Moses is "thick of tongue." What does that mean? Scholars are not sure, but many have identified it as some sort of speech pattern of slurring, mumbling, or even stuttering. Whatever it was, Moses was convinced that it disqualified him for the task God had assigned.

Let's pause here for just a moment and remember the phrase that I asked you to consider earlier in this chapter. Finish this sentence: O Lord,

I am not…. Don't skip this. Make sure you write your list at the end of this section. Share the things you "are not" with your family, friends, spouse, or small group. Whatever you do, tell God. Yes, He already knows. But you need to admit these things to Him, because it is very likely that the purpose God is calling you to will require you to get past what you can't do. As you name these things to God, consider his two answers to Moses in this story.

GOD'S RESPONSE # 1 TO WHAT YOU CAN'T DO:

I wonder if sometimes when we pray, God just wants to reply with a thundering, "DUH!" Of course God knew about Moses' speech deficiency. After all, as he asks rhetorically, "Who do you think made your mouth?" (My paraphrase.) We need to remember that whatever weakness we bring before the Lord, God already knows it. But our weaknesses and inabilities do not worry God at all. He doesn't try to reassure Moses with some "You can do it" pep talk. He simply says, "I will be with your mouth." Again, any "I am not" that you or I may lay before the Lord will always be answered with his assurance that he can use even that weakness.

With God, what we can't do just accentuates his strength. This is the lesson we will learn in a future chapter along with the apostle Paul. He actually says to Paul, "My power is made perfect in your weakness" (II Corinthians 12:9). You see, if Moses had been a master of language and an eloquent orator and debater, the delivery of God's people might have been credited to Moses. But when God takes a weak mouth and puts his word in it, his power is displayed clearly. This is true for us as well. You may not like it, and you may not believe it, but many times, the thing you can't do is what God will use to accomplish his purpose for your life.

GOD'S RESPONSE #2 TO WHAT YOU CAN'T DO:

Not only will God use what you can't do to accomplish his purpose in a powerful way, but his second response is that he will equip us with powerful resources to compensate for our weaknesses. Earlier in this encounter on the mountain, God had asked Moses, "What is that in your hand?" (Exodus 4:2). What was in Moses' hand was just an ordinary staff, but God decided to use a shepherd's tool as the visible symbol of his influence through Moses. This staff would turn into a snake, turn the Nile into blood, symbolically be stretched out to order each plague, and eventually part the Red Sea. God had literally put his own power into Moses' hand.

As great as we may think it would be to have this staff of God at our disposal, Jesus promised something much greater. In Acts chapter one, Christ addressed his closest followers, those who would be his witnesses to the known world. He told them to wait for his power to accompany them. "But you will receive power when the Holy Spirit has come upon you" (Acts 1:8). Better than a shepherd's staff that God has blessed with his power is the power of God living within each of us. And this is what each believer has with the Holy Spirit dwelling in us.

When we consider what we can't do, God says, "I will give you a representation of my power". To Moses he says, "What is in your hand?" But to us he says, "What is in you?" To accomplish his purpose in our lives, he has not given us a staff; he has given his Spirit to indwell us. He has given each of us his presence, power, and gifting through his Spirit. This is not just a tool for the few; all who follow Jesus by faith have his presence, power, and gifting inside of them. Let me encourage you this week to identify your Holy Spirit gifts through the resources recommended in the small group study at the end of this chapter. Write them down on the page provided. As you pray, you'll begin to see that God is most powerful in your weakness and that he will give you his Spirit to accomplish his purpose in you.

DAY TWENTY-THREE

Philip: Not enough

"Lifting up his eyes, then, and seeing that a large crowd was coming toward him, Jesus said to Philip, 'Where are we going to buy bread, so that these people may eat?' He said this to test him, for he himself knew what he would do. Philip answered him, 'Two hundred denarii worth of bread would not be enough for each of them to get a little.' One of his disciples, Andrew, Simon Peter's brother, said to him, 'There is a boy here who has five barley loaves and two fish, but what are they for so many?'" John 6:5-9

We don't like tests. Most sixteen-year-olds don't love the test that is required to get their driver's license. Who wants to drive while an instructor sits next to you grading your every move? Students don't enjoy taking lengthy tests in every class on finals week at the end of each semester. High school seniors are not fond of taking the hours-long ACT for a score that could determine their college future. University students get nervous about taking the comprehensive exams required to complete their degrees and graduate. This dislike for tests doesn't end with the educational years. Adults of all ages get apprehensive about their eye exams (*exam* is a cleverly disguised name for *test*). I've never heard someone with a heart issue say, "I'm really looking forward to my stress test tomorrow." Car owners dread the results of a diagnostic test on their car's engine. I could go on and on, but here's the truth: We don't like tests because we fear what they may reveal.

This is exactly why Jesus offers tests. His tests are not designed to embarrass us or give us failing grades, but to reveal something about our faith. Jesus' tests are not designed to discourage us, but to help us grow and discover what we really believe about him. His half- brother James actually says that we should embrace this spiritual testing, "[F]or you know that the testing of your faith produces steadfastness" (James 1:3). In other words, Jesus often puts our faith to the test to show us where it is lacking and to challenge us to increase our faith for the long run. When Jesus fed 5,000 people with five loaves and two fish, he gave a test to his disciples. He already knew what he was going to do, but he wanted to know if Philip and the others believed he could. It was a really short test with only one question, so let's take this faith exam today with our ancient brothers.

TEST QUESTION: HOW ARE WE GOING TO FEED ALL THESE PEOPLE?

John tells us that Jesus made this statement to test Philip, already knowing what he would do. Jesus knows he has power over all things. He knows the miracles he intends to work. He knows the resources he has at hand, and he always has a plan. What Jesus wanted to know on this occasion was what Philip (and the other disciples) thought he could do. This was a question of faith; it was not just about physical food. He wanted to know what they believed about his ability to fill those hungry stomachs so that in the future they would trust him to fill hungry souls. Did they believe that he is "the bread of life" (John 6:35) and "the bread that came down from heaven" (John 6:41)?

What test question is Jesus posing for us today? I don't think his question then and the one he's asking us now are that much different. How are we going to feed our entire hungry community? How are we going to share what we have with our closest friends and our acquaintances? How is this culture ever going to be spiritually satisfied? What will fill all of our junior and senior high schools with the love of Jesus? How will the whole world hear about Jesus? What can we do to feed the next generation the bread of life? What will it take to alleviate the inequalities and pain in the largest cities in America? How can we offer our families and coworkers the eternal nourishment of the gospel? How am I part of the answer to all the hungry people around me?

THE ANSWER: WE CAN'T

Jesus was asking a faith question, but Philip and Andrew turned it into a math question. Philip began by counting the people and then calculating the amount of money that would be needed to buy everyone's lunch--5,000 divided by 200 denarii = not enough. To his credit, Andrew seems to have done a search for food among the crowd, but all he could find was a little boy's lunch--five loaves and two fish < 5,000 lunches. They both gave math answers to a faith question, so they were both saying, "We can't." But it's Philip's response that we often mirror when faced with this week's question, "How can I?" We often fail the faith test, just as Philip did, because we think there "would not be enough."

This is the faith test for us today: What do we think we don't have enough of to live life *on purpose*? From a completely logical and human perspective, finish this sentence: I don't have enough _____. Maybe you are an older individual, and you think you don't have enough time. Maybe you are a younger person, and you think you don't have enough influence. Maybe you have limited resources, and you think you don't have enough money. It could be that you feel like there is not enough consensus or participation in your ministry. You might think that you don't have enough strength to do the job. Remember, Jesus is getting ready to do a miracle in your life. What is the limitation that your mind is clinging to?

THE RIGHT ANSWER: YOU CAN

Like looking in the teacher's edition of the math book, I'm going to give you the right answer. They should have looked at Jesus and said, "You are going to do a miracle, and we want to be used by you to help in any way that we can." You see, with Jesus, there is no such thing as "not enough." He can take whatever we have (even five loaves and two fish) and use it for his miraculous work, if we have faith. Jesus knows the miracle he is going to do in you. Can you get past what you don't have, or what little you have, and trust him to do it?

Remember your answer—it will be on the next test.

DAY TWENTY-FOUR

Paul: My grace is enough

"Three times I pleaded with the Lord about this, that it should leave me. But he said to me, 'My grace is sufficient for you, for my power is made perfect in weakness.' Therefore, I will boast all the more about my weaknesses, so that the power of Christ may rest upon me. For the sake of Christ then, I am content with weaknesses, insults, hardships, persecutions, and calamities. For when I am weak, then I am strong." (II Corinthians 12:8-10)

The Apostle Paul wrote half of the 27 books of the New Testament. He did innumerable miracles of healing in Jesus' name. He preached sermons that stirred entire cities to repentance. The Apostle Paul planted churches in every region of the known world. This man, formerly named Saul, had a supernatural meeting with Jesus and found his calling on the road to Damascus. This first-century world changer organized a missionary network of church leaders and workers. One could argue for Peter, but there was probably no greater influence in the first-century church than the Apostle Paul. So it would seem that Jesus would answer Paul's request and take away his "thorn in the flesh" (II Corinthians 12:7). But Jesus didn't!

What exactly was this "thorn in the flesh" that Paul referred to? There are many possible biblical and historical theories. A very strong case can be made, from Paul's letter to the Galatians, for some sort of eye problem. When writing to the believers in Galatia, he said, "You know it was because of a bodily ailment that I preached the gospel to you at the first" (Galatians 4:13) and a few verses later added, "[I]f possible, you would have gouged out your eyes and given them to me" (Galatians 4:15). He also commented, "See with what large letters I am writing to you with my own hand" (Galatians 6:11). Perhaps his thorn was bad eyesight.

Others conjecture that his thorn was some sort of chronic pain. He certainly had suffered physical injuries. He had been beaten many times. He had spent nights in appalling and unsanitary jails. He had traveled countless miles on land and been shipwrecked at sea. And now, as an old man, he probably had unceasing pain. These documented traumas, and our current understanding that health issues often cause mental and emotional distress, mean that Paul may have dealt with depression and despair as well. Many have assigned some sort of sin or temptation to this thorn, but this is a hard biblical argument to make because he asked God to take it away… and God would never refuse to take away a sin or temptation. In the end, his summary of "weaknesses, insults, hardships, persecutions, and calamities" pretty much sums it up. He likened his "thorn in the flesh" to physical, emotional, mental, and even spiritual pain. But why would God not take it away? Three reasons may help us understand why he allows pain to continue in our lives.

OUR WEAKNESSES ARE OFTEN "A MESSENGER OF SATAN TO HARASS US"

It is easy to forget that we are in a cosmic, spiritual battle and that for every victory we celebrate in Jesus, Satan is there to bring harm to those who serve him. I'm not trying to be an alarmist, but I must be biblical. Satan is scheming against us (Ephesians 6:11), roaring to devour us (I Peter 4:8), and is waging war against us (Revelation 12:17). If we live our lives *on purpose* for our King Jesus, we should expect the ruler of the opposing kingdom to use everything in his power to harass and harm us. Following Jesus is *not*, I repeat, is *not* an easy road. God does not keep us from harm, always bring us financial prosperity, or bring worldly success to all his followers. If he does, he has a lot of explaining to do to the Apostle Paul.

Day Twenty-Four

OUR WEAKNESSES KEEP US FROM BECOMING CONCEITED

Paul admitted that he had seen some pretty remarkable things, including visions of heaven and revelations from the Lord. He even acknowledged that he was boasting to share such things. Many scholars believe he was referring to his supernatural conversion experience (II Corinthians 12:1-5). Whether that is true or not, Paul was obviously called by God, empowered by God, and was doing great things for God. This is a hard lesson, but one we must embrace: If Paul had lived free from pain, succeeded in every ministry venture, had no relational conflict, and been financially solvent, he would have been tempted to take credit for all of it. This is the reality of humankind. When things are going well, we tend to think it's because we're so great. Sometimes, God allows us to endure pain to keep us humble and reliant on him.

OUR WEAKNESSES ARE OFTEN THE WAY GOD'S POWER IS MADE PERFECT

Finally, and perhaps most importantly, the star of the show in living a life *on purpose* must be God's power, not ours. The upside down economy of the kingdom of God is that the weak are the strongest. The least are the greatest. The last are first. This was demonstrated perfectly in the person of Jesus Christ. He became a servant to become master of all. He submitted to death so that all may live. He became weak to exhibit his power. He was buried so that he could conquer the grave. Jesus stayed on the cross to show his authority over sin. Jesus washed his disciples' feet to model humble leadership. Jesus was silent at his trial so that the heavens could roar his victory. He knelt so that every knee would bow to him.

What are your weaknesses? If you're like me, you can easily identify emotional, physical, mental, and spiritual "thorns" that you'd rather not have. By Jesus' command, and the Spirit's presence within you, you have been given the right to ask the Father to take them away. It's always appropriate to appeal to his mercy. But don't be surprised if he answers you as he did Paul. His grace of saving you through Jesus is enough. And while you may wish he would use your strengths to fulfill his purpose in you, he may prefer to use your weaknesses. For when we are weak, he is strong.

DAY TWENTY-FIVE

Zerubbabel: By my Spirit

"Then he said to me, 'This is the word of the Lord to Zerubbabel: Not by might, nor by power, but by my Spirit, says the Lord of hosts. Who are you, O great mountain? Before Zerubbabel you shall become a plain. And he shall bring forward the top stone amid shouts of 'Grace, grace to it.'" (Zechariah 4:6&7)

One of the toughest things to navigate in a life lived *on purpose* for God is the.................. timing. See what I did there? Often, God's call to his work is clear, but he doesn't reveal the exact timetable for accomplishing it. For example, when God told Abraham to go to the land he would show him and declared that he would make him the father of many nations, he didn't reveal that it would be 25 years before Abraham and Sarah would have their son of promise, Isaac. This was also the lesson learned by our Old Testament brother Zerubbabel. God clearly called him, along with the high priest Jeshua, to return to Jerusalem to lead in rebuilding the temple and restoring worship (see Ezra 3:1-9). But it was twenty-four years before his calling became reality. To understand Zerubbabel's story, we need some historical background.

In 587 BC, King Nebuchadnezzar laid siege to Jerusalem for two years, left it in ruins, destroyed the temple, and took thousands of Jews to Babylon. Among the captives was the last king to sit on Jerusalem's throne, King Jehoiachin, Zerubbabel's grandfather. In 539 BC, Cyrus the Great, whose Persian Empire had conquered Babylon, decreed that Jewish exiles could return home and Zerubbabel was among those who returned (Ezra

2:2). Not only did he return, but as a royal descendant to the Jewish throne, he was made a governor of Judaea under Cyrus' authority. He was charged with rebuilding the temple in Jerusalem that had been destroyed in 586. After years of exile, Zerubbabel must have sensed God's great purpose and calling in his life. Instead of being a king in exile, God would use him to reestablish the throne of King David and the dignity of his people.

After the first year back in Jerusalem, Zerubbabel had overseen completion of the foundation of the temple, and the newly-returned exiles had celebrated Passover for the first time in years. Our hero must have felt pretty good about how he was answering God's call. Then opposition arose, and the construction abruptly stopped as local opponents of the Jewish people wrote letters of criticism and warning to the king. To complicate things further, it was a time of transition in the Persian Empire because King Cyrus died, and a succession of kings followed on the throne there. God's purpose for Zerubbabel in Jerusalem was on hold until 520 BC, 18 years after he had returned. By then, he was under the authority of King Darius, whom he did not know.

What happens when you face a mountain of challenges like those described in our verses for today? Zerubbabel wanted to live *on purpose*, but the obstacles of opposition and politics blocked his way. What was he to do? He could have led his people in rebellion against the emperor. He could have continued the work and attempted to ignore the enemies' hostility. He could have fought against and silenced his opponents. Or he could have abandoned the work completely and pursued another plan for his life. Instead, God spoke to him through the prophet Zechariah, whose words speak to us as well.

There are times, even in the midst of *on purpose* living for Jesus, when mountains obstruct our path. For Zerubbabel, the barriers were direct opposition and his lack of authority. What is your biggest obstacle for living out God's calling in your life? For some, personal health stands in the way. For others, it's emotional baggage or pain from the past. Some may be facing a mountain of financial debt, the disruption of broken relationships, or the challenges of caring for family members. We spend so much of our time trying to fix these things using our own power and strength. But God has a better plan for us, just as he did for our ancient brother. Through the prophet Zechariah, God told Zerubbabel the same thing he still reminds us of today: You won't finish the work I have for you by your might or your power, however powerful or mighty you are. No—God's work will always be accomplished through the power of his Spirit. God is neither scared of the powers that rise against us, nor is he impressed with the power of those he has called. When God calls us to live *on purpose,* he gives us the power of his Spirit to accomplish that purpose and to accomplish it at just the right time.

I'm guessing that during the 18-year hiatus from living out his purpose, there were days when Zerubbabel had all but given up on his calling to rebuild the temple. But God hadn't given up. Through the prophet, he assured this man that he would complete the task. The mountain of opposition would become a plain, and Zechariah even predicted that the people would shout "Grace, grace to it" as the final stone was put into place. The temple was finished in 515 BC and was forever known as Zerubbabel's temple. Historically, even though Herod the Great enhanced the temple in the early First century AD, the "second temple period" is always a reference to the work of this man, Zerubbabel, who fulfilled his God-given purpose for him.

God is still building his temple in us today. The foundation has been laid on the cornerstone, Jesus Christ (I Corinthians 3:11). God has begun a good work in us, and he will complete it (Philippians 1:6). We are his workmanship, having been empowered by his Spirit to do the good work he has called us to do (Ephesians 2:10). In the end, the temple of God that is the church *will* be finished—just like the one Zerubbabel built. Then, the shout of all God's people will be "Grace!" God will accomplish all he plans to do in us by his grace, through Jesus, the grace to save us, the grace to use us, and the grace to bring us eternally home.

DAY TWENTY-SIX

HOLY SPIRIT: His gift for me

"Now concerning spiritual gifts, brothers [and sisters], I do not want you to be uninformed. Now, there are a variety of gifts, but the same Spirit; and there are varieties of service, but the same Lord; and there are varieties of activities, but it is the same God who empowers them all in everyone. To each is given the manifestation of the Spirit for the common good. All these are empowered by one and the same Spirit, who apportions to each one individually as he wills. God arranged the members of the body, each one of them, as he chose." (I Corinthians 12:1, 4-7, 11, 18).

Here is where our journey towards living life *on purpose* picks up speed. Over the last several weeks we have confronted our thoughts of unworthiness and lack of qualifications. We have noted our weaknesses and have addressed our limitations. But like Zerubbabel in the last chapter, it often feels as if we don't have enough power to overcome obstacles and be used by and for God. God knows all of this. For every reason we give for not being able to live *on purpose* for God, he extends a greater calling and confirms how he has empowered us. He has placed his Holy Spirit in every Christ-follower so that we can accomplish his specific will and purpose. This is not a cookie-cutter one-size-fits-all calling. Through the Holy Spirit, God has an individual plan for every believer. I'm praying that today and tomorrow you will find your gift and find your place. Let's begin with your spiritual gift(s).

THERE ARE A VARIETY OF GIFTS
GIVEN BY THE HOLY SPIRIT

The church in Corinth was enamored with the supernatural Holy Spirit gift of speaking in tongues. We know that the Holy Spirit's presence was evident on the first day of the church when the apostles "began to speak in other tongues" (Acts 2:4). This may not be as crazy or spectacular as you might think. The Greek word *glossas*, usually translated as tongues, simply means "languages." By the power of the Spirit, these uneducated Galileans were able to speak in the languages of the 13 nations represented in Jerusalem on that day. There also seems to be a Holy Spirit prayer language that Paul acknowledges in Acts 14:2. We don't have time to address this issue completely now, but in the next chapter we'll address the purpose of speaking in tongues and the purpose of all gifts. The point is that the Corinthians desired the supernatural, miraculous, and visible gifts of the Spirit above the other gifts.

But that's not how it works. There is great variety in the gifts that the Holy Spirit gives. Here Paul mentions wisdom, knowledge, faith, healing, miracles, prophecy, etc… (I Corinthians 12:8-10). In the Bible, there are four passages commonly referenced when examining the variety of gifts that the Holy Spirit gives. A compilation from Romans 12:6-8, I Corinthians 12:8-10, I Peter 4:10-11, and Ephesians 4:11 offers 21 unique gifts of the Spirit. In my studies I have come to understand that these are not exhaustive lists. God's Spirit does not limit himself to such a small number of gifts when there are so many activities and so much service to be accomplished in the church. And though many spiritual gift assessments (like the one we're encouraging you to take from this week's small group study notes) often sort us all into 21 gift categories, I believe that there are thousands of Holy Spirit gifts given to the church.

TO EACH IS GIVEN THE MANIFESTATION OF THE SPIRIT

The next thing Paul wanted to tell these Corinthians about spiritual gifts was that everyone has a gift, not just those whose gifts are more public or visible than others. This is important because in the church we are tempted to think of the worship leaders, the preachers, and the group and ministry leaders as the ones who are "gifted." But this is not the teaching of Scripture. The Bible is clear that every Christian has Spirit-manifested gifts. Who is gifted? Those who pray for leaders daily at home. Those who sit on the floor and teach three-year-olds. Those who run sound, program computers, mop floors, set up chairs, shovel snow, mow grass, manage finances, write lessons, produce videos, change diapers in the nursery, and write cards to people in times of pain. I have witnessed all of these and many others being expressed by Spirit-gifted Christians in a supernatural way. If you are a Christ-follower, you have been given spiritual gifts.

EACH ONE IS DESIGNED AS GOD HAS CHOSEN

Finally, certain gifts are given to you with great intentionality to fulfill God's specific purpose through you. We may be tempted to think, "I wish I had another gift, or a better gift, or a bigger gift." Such thinking misses the care that God took to create us uniquely for who we are in Jesus. Do you remember that after everything God created in Genesis 1, he said the words "it is good"? Do you also remember that when he created humankind, he said "it is *very* good"? (Genesis1:31). Well, in Jesus we are new creations (II Corinthians 5:17) and by the design of his Holy Spirit he has chosen the gift(s) we have received. And that is very good. As we end this chapter, let me encourage you to prayerfully consider four questions that will help you understand your Holy Spirit gift.

- Is there something you do for Jesus or his church that really makes you come alive?

- Is there an area of service for Jesus or his church that others frequently affirm you for and comment on?

- Is there something you do in your Christ-following service and it doesn't matter to you if anyone sees, acknowledges, or gives you credit for doing it?

- Is there something you do for Jesus or his church that has eternal implications for others?

- We're getting closer…to living *on purpose.*

DAY TWENTY-SEVEN

THE BODY: His place for me

"For just as the body is one and has many members, and all the members of the body, though many, are one body, so it is with Christ. For the body does not consist of one member but of many. If the foot should say, 'Because I am not a hand, I do not belong to the body', that would not make it any less part of the body. And if the ear should say, 'Because I am not an eye, I do not belong to the body,' that would not make it any less a part of the body. If the whole body were an eye, where would be the sense of hearing? If the whole body were an ear, where would be the sense of smell? But as it is, God arranged the members of the body, each one of them, as he chose. If all were a single member, where would the body be? As it is, there are many body parts, yet one body." (I Corinthians 12:12, 14-20).

Quick anatomy test—no right answer—first thing that pops into your mind. Ready? What is your most important body part? If you're like most people, you probably answered with one of the "life essential" organs, like brain, heart, or lungs. Or you may have gone the practical route and thought of your eyes, feet, or hands. It would be hard to argue against any of these vital body parts being important. But now, let's reverse the question. Ready? What is your least important body part? Many of us probably thought about the spleen, wisdom teeth, appendix, or fingernails. Did anyone answer nose hairs? (I'm asking for a friend.) For some of us this was a harder question than the first one because frankly, there are dozens of unimportant body parts that we seldom think about. This may seem like a silly exercise, but it gets us to the heart of the metaphor Paul uses to explain our place in the church, the body of Christ.

In the last chapter, we identified the way in which the Holy Spirit has gifted each Christ-follower with a specific and God-selected spiritual gift. So now that we have discovered our gift, we have to find our place. And according to the apostle, our place is as a part of the body of Jesus, the church. In the same way that the human body is made up of various parts, so is the church. "For just as the body is one and has many members… so it is with Christ" (I Corinthians 12:12). So what body part do you see yourself as in the body of Christ? When I asked this question of students back in my youth ministry days, I got all kinds of answers. Most either tried to identify a part that matched their personality (e.g., "I'm the knee because I'm flexible" or "I'm a hand because I like to draw") or say something obscure or funny (e.g., "probably a pinky toe," "I'd be a freckle on the back," or "a callous on the big toe"). Well, whatever body part you see yourself as, let's consider these important church-anatomy truths from I Corinthians 12 that apply to every body part.

EVERY BODY PART BELONGS

Paul humorously described a scenario in which a body part would actually question whether or not it belonged, based on what it was *not*. While none of us has actually witnessed our foot or ear expressing an existential crisis like the ones in I Corinthians 12, I can tell you that there are many in the church who think and feel this way. And even though gaining a sense of belonging is hard in just about every social circle, club, friend group, or organizations, by the blood of Jesus, belonging is never in question in the body of Christ. All who follow Jesus by faith have the gift of the Holy Spirit living in them, and this means that they belong. This is so important because when you find the place where you belong, you can live *on purpose*. Here is the truth: Without Jesus, life is just one big search for belonging, but in him you find your place in his love and in his church. This brings us to the next truth.

EVERY BODY PART NEEDS THE OTHERS

Obviously, there are body parts that seem more important than others, but no body part can survive without the others. Any great running strategy the brain can concoct is going to take feet, legs, and lungs to win the race. Shoveling the snow is going to take both hands, back muscles (trust me), and a beating heart to clear the driveway. Completing a project on the computer will depend on eyes seeing images, the brain processing information, fingers pushing keys, and a posterior sitting in the seat.

It's the same way in the body of the church. "God has so composed the body... that members have the same care for one another" (I Corinthians 12:25). Let me say it another way: We depend on each other to fully function as the body of Christ. For the body to grow, it takes teachers, rockers (in the nursery and on the stage), prayers, servers, encouragers, builders, sowers (evangelists, but people who sew, too) and planners, to name a few. Without all of the body parts functioning as they are designed to, the work of the body becomes exponentially harder. There are many reasons I can think of for Christ-followers to be regularly involved in the church, but the most important one is that when you don't show up for corporate worship, small group, or serving teams, it's as if an ear, hand, or eye is missing. Can the body still function? Technically, yes. But clearly not as well. Living *on purpose* is so crucial because the whole body is depending on every part to do its part. One more thing.

EVERY BODY PART IS THERE FOR THE OTHERS

Body parts are there for each other in good and bad times. What happens when there's an injury to the body? What happens when the pinky toe gets stubbed, or the arm gets broken, the eye gets something in it, or the mind gets discouraged? God has designed the body to do two things: heal and compensate. By God's design, when pain or an injury happens in our physical bodies, there are bodily functions that immediately begin a healing process (like tear ducts when our eyes are irritated). Not only does the body work to heal itself, but the body parts that are not damaged pick up the slack for others (like using your arms to walk on crutches as your leg heals).

The body of Jesus is the same. Sometimes parts of the body of Christ are injured with a career failure, a cancer diagnosis, a baby's prognosis, or the death of a loved one. In those moments, the church body is designed to help with the healing and fill in the gaps for those who are struggling. Personally, my small groups, my staff, my elders, and my congregation have literally healed my heart and made up for my weakness as I have experienced our grandson dealing with the effects of chronic kidney failure. I have preached and worked when I was injured, but hundreds of you—the body parts of this church—have picked me up in my weakness, prayed for me, and strengthened me for God's glory. That's how the body works. Each member is there for the others.

Find your place in the body. You belong. You are needed. Together with all the other body parts, we are one in Christ.

DAY TWENTY-EIGHT

JESUS: Sympathy for our weaknesses

"Since then we have a great high priest who has passed through the heavens, Jesus, the son of God, let us hold fast our confession. For we do not have a high priest who is unable to sympathize with our weaknesses, but one who in every respect has been tempted as we are, yet without sin. Let us then with confidence draw near to the throne of grace, that we might receive mercy and find grace to help in time of need" (Hebrews 4:14-16).

"You just don't understand" is a line that has been used by just about every teenager who has ever lived. I said it to my parents, my kids said it to me, and my grandchildren will someday say it to my kids. This statement implies that there are circumstances in the teen's life that no parent could possibly understand and that keep their elders from responding in a logical and loving way. Most of the time, this accusation is not accurate. For example, "The reason you won't let me see my boyfriend or girlfriend is because you don't understand what it's like to be in love." Or "You won't let me go on spring break with my friends because you don't know how important friendships are in high school." Well kids, believe it or not, we old parents and grandparents were once in love and even had friends. LOL

However, sometimes the "You just don't understand" sentiment is truer now than we realize. I think there are unique pressures that this generation of teens and young adults are experiencing that are hard for those of us in older generations to understand. Their accusation that we don't understand the pressure they are under to achieve, how exposed they are to sexual content, and how the constant barrage of incoming information has overloaded their psyches is probably accurate. In this fast-paced society, many teens struggle with depression and mental illness, and unless they share their burdens, it's often true that we "just don't understand."

This is why this generation and every generation needs the love of Jesus. We need someone who understands us. Every bit of us. All of our heart's desires. All that our minds take in, and all that we hope for, long for, and are fearful of. We need someone who knows exactly what it feels like to be us. We need someone who has walked in our shoes, lived in our world, and experienced all of our messes. His name is Jesus. We can never say "You just don't understand" to him because as today's reading points out, he does.

HE UNDERSTANDS WHAT IT FEELS LIKE TO BE WEAK

The verses we are studying today are written about Jesus' role as high priest. They make it clear that he is not a spiritual elitist who is unable to relate to the people he leads. He is able to sympathize with our weaknesses. The word *sympathy* is translated from the Greek word *sumpatheo--sum* [with] and *patheo* [to feel], meaning literally "to feel with." What are your weaknesses? When Jesus poured himself out through the incarnation to become human, he became subject to our mortal weaknesses. He got thirsty, hungry, tired, sprained his ankle, got poison ivy, and had a runny nose, just as we do. Because he walked the earth as a man, he knows what it feels like when a loved one dies; he cried at his friend Lazarus' funeral (John 11). He knows what it's like to be poor because he grew up in one of the poorest parts of Israel. He knows about family issues. He lived with his family's unbelief and their effort to take him away because they thought he was crazy (Mark 3:21). He knows what it feels like when a friend betrays you (Judas) and a best friend doesn't stand up for you (Peter). He knows what it feels like when your friends abandon you (the disciples in the garden and at the cross). He knows loneliness. He even knows the anguish of the mind that could be labeled depression or anxiety: "His soul was very sorrowful, even to death" (Matthew 26:38). You may say a lot of things about Jesus, but you can't say that he doesn't understand your weaknesses. But there's more.

103

HE UNDERSTANDS WHAT IT FEELS LIKE TO BE TEMPTED

Satan's temptation of Jesus in the wilderness is recorded in each of the first three gospels of the New Testament. It's as if the Holy Spirit didn't want us to miss the reality that he was tempted just as we are. He was tempted to feed his appetite (turn stones to bread), to gain all the world's kingdoms (bow down to Satan), and show off his God power (throw yourself off of the temple). Yet each time, Jesus did not sin. And that ended Satan's tricks, right? No. You and I have learned that overcoming temptation once doesn't mean there won't be future temptations. This was true for Jesus, and it is true for us.

I've always been intrigued by this line in the Bible: "And when the devil had ended every temptation, he departed from him *until an opportune time"* (Luke 4:13, italics mine). Does the phrase "ended every temptation" indicate only the three we know about, or were there other temptations that the gospel writers didn't record for us? After all, Jesus was "…in the wilderness for forty days being tempted by the devil" (Luke 4:1b-2a). But this is not the most important part of this passage. Jesus didn't face temptation just once in the wilderness and then never again. He faced temptation over and over and over. Every time Satan saw an opportunity to lure Jesus to sin, he bombarded him with visual images, thoughts, and evil ideas. Every temptation we will ever face was pressed onto Jesus as well. Even…? Yes, even that. Unlike us, he remained sinless, but we can be confident that he understands all of our temptations.

What does all of this mean as we close a week of considering our own limitations? It means that we can turn to someone, the only ONE, who truly understands every enticement of the devil. We can turn to Jesus for mercy in our time of need and know, without any doubt, that he cares. This is what separates the God of Christianity from all others. He is not indifferent and haughty in some far-off eternal place wondering what's wrong with us. He knows that sin is what's wrong with us. That's why he became one of us. It is only in Christ that we begin to find the strength to overcome our pain, our weaknesses, and our temptations. In the meanwhile, turn to him for help in every circumstance--because he gets it.

HOW CAN I?
EXODUS 4:10-12

Days 22-28

Moses had been given the exact gifts that God wanted him to have. Each one was designed to be used for God's glory. The hardest lesson for Moses during this burning bush experience was to shift his focus from what he could not do to what God could do. This is a crucial example for us: our perceived shortcomings never limit God's ability to use us. God challenges us to look past our inabilities and weaknesses and trust him for our Holy Spirit-given gifts and abilities. When you and I acknowledge how God has gifted us, we are ready to live on purpose.

Let's get started. . .

1. Discuss your Sunday sermon notes and highlights from the Day Twenty-Two reading. Be sure to note any questions or challenges that arise.

2. Watch this week's video "How Can I?" As you watch, write down key phrases, and write an answer to Mike's question. "I am not: _____."

3. Spend some time reviewing the daily devotionals from this week. Which day's chapter was the most useful in helping you understand your gifts?

4. Living on purpose helps us put our weaknesses into perspective. Day Twenty-Eight reminds us that Jesus knows everything that we are going through in our lives. Because of this, we can have complete confidence in how he's gifted us. Share a time when God carried you through a situation where you felt weak and lacking in the gifts you needed.

5. As a group exercise, take the spiritual gifts assessment found at www.eastview.church/mygifts. Allow enough time for each group member to share one or two of their top gifts. Consider these questions from your own perspective, and allow group members to share what they see in you:

   • How do you see these gifts in your life?

   • Where are your gifts most "alive," most on display?

   • What obstacles or excuses hold you back from confidently using your gifts?

6. Read Exodus 4:10-12 together. What is the promise that God gave Moses? Even if it feels awkward, take turns speaking verse 12 over one another. Let this be both a prayer and a blessing that you share sincerely.

Ok, so now what. . .

Final Takeaway. . . What is one way you will you use your gift on purpose this week?

_____

_____

_____

Next Steps. . .

- Apply your takeaway.

- Learn more about your gifts and how you can genuinely use them for the kingdom.

- Keep reading and talking with others about what God is doing.

For Further Reflection. . .

- There are a number of great spiritual gift assessments. We have provided one for you through Eastview's website. We also highly recommend another one that looks at the five spiritual gifts found in Ephesians 4. Go to https://5qcentral.com/tests or check out the week 4 section in the appendix for this resource and other ways to further your study of this week's theme.

DAY TWENTY-NINE

Can You Send Someone Else?

"But he said, 'Oh, my Lord, please send someone else.'
Then the anger of the Lord was kindled against Moses
and he said, 'Is there not Aaron, your brother, the
Levite? I know that he can speak well. Behold, he is
coming out to meet you, and when he sees you, he will
be glad in his heart. You shall speak to him and put
words in his mouth, and I will be with your mouth
and with his mouth and will teach you both what to
do. He shall speak for you to the people, and he shall
be your mouth, and you shall be his God. And take in
your hand this staff, with which you shall do signs.'"
Exodus 4:13-17

Before we get to our question for today, I want to introduce you to a word, or give you a better understanding of a word that you may already know. The word is *synergy*. It comes from a compound Greek word: *sunergos*. The prefix *sun* is usually translated as *with*, and the word *ergos* usually becomes our English word *work*. When you put these two together, you get a simple translation meaning "with work"—the idea of working together. So our word *synergy* means "to work together." But that is just the literal definition.

Scientifically, synergy is impressive because it increases output exponentially. This means that the combined effect of two working together is greater than the sum of its parts. Let me illustrate with an example. One of the world's biggest and strongest horses is the Belgian draft horse. In annual competitions, each horse is able to pull as much as 8,000 pounds. But here's the fascinating thing—when you harness two of these horses together, you would expect they could pull 16,000 pounds, right? Well, that's good math, but bad science. By working together (synergy), these two horses that can pull 8,000 pounds each, then pull as much as 24,000 pounds as a team! The output of the two horses working together is three times as much as working alone. Moses will soon find comfort in this reality for himself.

As we eavesdrop once again on the mountain conversation between God and Moses, we assume that Moses has accepted his purpose and is ready, willing, and able to go and do what God has called him to do. He knows where he is, who God is, who he is (and is not), and what God is going to do powerfully through him. All he has to do now is pack up and follow God, *on purpose*, into Egypt. But Moses is still not ready. He has one more question for God and this may be the most surprising question of all. At this point, he can't say he doesn't know God's purpose for his life. His questions and God's answers have made that abundantly clear. Now it's a question of willingness…and Moses is just not willing to go. So he blurts out, "Can you send someone else?" (Exodus 4:13).

Why was Moses unwilling to go? The Bible doesn't tell us what's going on in his heart, so we can't be sure. But we can make some educated spiritual guesses based on the reasons *we* are often unwilling to live *on purpose* for God. I don't think Moses lacked faith in who God was. Their conversation was undeniably a *holy ground* moment. The burning bush and the miraculous qualities of Moses' staff would make it impossible to deny God's presence and power. This doesn't seem to be a willful and obstinate disobedience either. In fact, Moses doesn't say, "I'm not going." He just asks God if he could send someone else. So why was Moses looking for a way out? I think there are two main reasons, and I've seen them both in my life and in the lives of those I serve with.

LIVING "ON PURPOSE" WILL BE HARD

It's quite possible that as God was revealing his purpose for him, Moses was considering what a difficult assignment this was going to be. Traveling the 200 miles across the desert will be hard for an eighty-year-old man.

He's not the vigorous forty-year-old he was when he ran from the Egyptian authorities. Leading people—even the people of God—will not be easy. They will second-guess his directions, question his calling, accuse him of bringing them harm, and be angry enough to kill him. And harder yet will be the opposition and threats that Moses knows will come from Pharaoh and his officials. When he asked God to send someone else, he may have been thinking, "I'm not up for such hard work."

Living *on purpose* should come with this warning label: Just because God has chosen, gifted, and equipped you for his work, it doesn't mean it will be easy. Let me be clear—living *on purpose* for God will always be hard work. When gifted people live *on purpose* in the kingdom of God, it may look easy to others because God has called them to it. It's not. I know people who are passionate about special needs ministry; it's not easy. Our community center and food pantry staff and volunteers are called to serve there, but it's hard work. Leading a junior high small group? Not easy. Leading worship. Leading a small group. Keeping the church building clean. Working in the nursery. All of these and a million more ministries in Jesus' name are hard work.

LIVING *ON PURPOSE* WILL COST YOU

Moses may have been thinking not only of the difficulty of the task but also of the cost of the task. The cost to do what God wanted him to do would be great. It would be expensive to get supplies ready for the trip ahead. It was going to cost him his shepherding career, the income it provided, and the leisure of retirement. Going to Egypt would cost him family time and the 40-year-long relationships he had established in Midian. And at this point, Moses probably had no idea that he was being asked to commit to working for another 40 years (the rest of his life).

Living *on purpose* will cost us as well. This has always been the case for Christ-followers. Jesus even warned his early followers to "count the cost" of discipleship to him. Most of us who lean into the purpose that we discover in this study will invest time, resources, and energy into our calling. Some, like many believers before them, will leave careers, home, comfort, country, and family in order to follow God's purpose for them.

I think there are many of us who wish God would send someone else for all of the reasons stated above.

Before we get to the Lord's solution for how hard and costly living *on purpose* may be, let's look at his reaction to Moses' unwillingness. His anger burned against Moses! And who could blame him? Second only to willful sin and disobedience, I would guess that nothing angers the Lord more than the reluctance of his people to follow his call on their lives. I wonder how many times God has opened doors, nudged us by his Spirit, miraculously answered prayers, and shown his power in our lives only to hear us say, "Can you just send someone else?" Thankfully, the Lord works, even in our reluctance, to accomplish his will. He does this by pairing us with others who have gifts we don't have so that we can work together, *on purpose*, to accomplish his eternal will and bring his kingdom to earth. God's response to Moses reveals a key for living life *on purpose*. "Yes Moses, I will send someone else... WITH you!"

I believe Moses' greatest hesitancy was that he didn't want to carry out this purpose by himself. I also believe God's plan had always been to send Aaron with Moses. "Is there not Aaron, your brother, the Levite? I know that he can speak well. Behold, he is coming to meet you..." (Exodus 4:14). When you pair this statement with God's call to Aaron in Exodus 4:27, it appears that God has commanded Aaron to meet Moses in the wilderness. In other words, God was going to accomplish his will using Moses' gifts in combination with Aaron's gifts. Their individual purposes were going to be realized in community.

As we consider our own purpose, here's what you need to know. God never calls his followers to live *on purpose* by themselves. Jesus called twelve, not one. Jesus sent them out two by two, not one by one. In Acts 13 we read, "The Holy Spirit said, 'Set apart for me Barnabas and Saul for the work to which I have called them.'" (verse 2). By God's design, following and serving him in the church is a team sport. The church is one body made up of many parts. Your purpose will not be found in solitude. It will always come in the context of the people of God and your place within the church body.

In I Corinthians 3:9, the apostle Paul uses that word we mentioned at the beginning of the chapter. He says there, speaking of himself, Apollos, and Peter, "For we are God's fellow workers (*sunergos*)." Paul didn't see himself as a one-man super apostle who could go it alone. He had discovered, with Moses, that his purpose could be fully expressed only by working together with others whose gifts complimented and enhanced his own for the glory of God. At the end of Romans 16, Paul names many people as his *sunergos* or "fellow workers" (see Romans 16:3,9, and 21). Let's do the same. At the end of this section, write down the names of your fellow workers, the people in your life whose gifts compliment yours and multiply God's work exponentially. This is the synergy that Moses found with Aaron, that Paul found with Timothy, and that we find with each other.

DAY THIRTY

Love one another

"A new commandment I give to you, that you love one another: just as I have loved you, you also are to love one another. By this all people will know that you are my disciples if you have love for one another. This is my commandment, that you love one another as I have loved you. These things have I commanded you, so that you will love one another" (John 13:34&35, 15:12&17).

I'm a sports fan from Indiana who has spent most of my life in central Illinois. That means that my next declaration will not be accepted favorably by most of my brothers and sisters as they read this book. Brace yourselves--I'm an Indiana University basketball fan. I can actually hear your "boos" from where I am right now. Still, I'm an all-in, "Hurryin' Hoosiers," "Indiana we're all for you," "Go IU," "mop lady" fan. If you're from Indiana you get it. If you aren't, you don't (especially the mop lady thing). But something strange has happened to my favorite sports school in the past few years. It has turned into a football school! For most of my life, football has taken a back seat (like the way-back seat in the family minivan) to Indiana basketball. But these days, football is gaining. The basketball team hasn't been much to brag about lately, and the football team is winning! Much of IU's success on the gridiron can be attributed to Coach Tom Allen and his use of a simple three letter encouragement: LEO.

You can hashtag it (#LEO) if you want. It's definitely a thing, but it's what these letters stand for that I'm interested in. This football coach, in a game that historically has included profane language and in-your-face screaming,

113

is encouraging his team simply to Love Each Other. Not everyone is buying into Coach Allen's approach. In fact, I heard one commentator make fun of the notion that love could win a game. His perspective was that the team members' love for each other wouldn't matter when they faced a team with superior football skill. That comment was made right before this team that focuses on love almost pulled off one of the greatest upsets ever against a much more talented opponent. Maybe love *could* win football games. More importantly, according to Jesus, love wins the day in his church.

"Love one another" didn't originate with a football coach. It started with our savior, Jesus, and was commanded the very night he was betrayed. During his final hours with his followers, he taught about love and said, "Greater love has no one than this; that someone lay down his life for his friends" (John 15:13). He didn't just command his disciples to love one another, he led by example by washing their feet and then by giving his life for their sakes. They had no idea what Jesus was facing that night long ago, but his heartfelt words stayed with them and love became, and has continued to be, the dominant message of the church for nearly 2,000 years. At Eastview, in our Vision Statement, we call this "ridiculous love." We recognize that the love of Jesus doesn't make sense to the world. It didn't in his time, and it doesn't in ours. His instructions were ridiculed (this is where we get our word *ridiculous* from) by the ancient pagan-Roman world. What kind of God *dies* for the love of those inferior to him? Jesus did. And he commands his followers to love sacrificially too.

Jesus called this a new commandment because to his rule-following and law-observing Jewish contemporaries, it sounded very different from their familiar Old Testament restrictions. But Jesus, God in the flesh, knew that in fact every rule, every law, and every command is about love at its core. Jesus said it this way, "You shall *love* the Lord your God with all your heart and with all your soul and with all your mind. This is the great and first commandment. And a second is like it: You shall *love* your neighbor as yourself. On these two commandments depend *all the Law and the Prophets*" (Matthew 22:37-40, italics mine). God has always been reaching out to his people in love. This is why Jesus tells his followers to love one another.

First, we are to love one another because he has loved us. Look at Eastview's understanding of the "ridiculous love" of Jesus. It is ridiculous to love someone who can't love you fully, can't add value to who you are, and who may reject your love. But this is what God did for us through Jesus. When Jesus says, "Love one another as I have loved you," he is telling us to love one another in a sacrificial way. Don't think that the call to love other Christians is easy. Christians can be as hard to love as non-Christians. They often don't deserve to be loved for what they have done or said. They are sometimes unlovely or unlovable. Christ-followers don't always love you back. But this is where we are different from the world. We can love people like this because Jesus loved people like us.

Second, we are to love one another because this points others to the one we follow. Jesus could have chosen many things that would mark his church and identify those who were his disciples. He could have said, "Let's be known for our wisdom." After all, Jesus was God's true and right word incarnated, and he passed his words on to us. He could have encouraged us to be known for supernatural miracles or for his powerful accomplishments, and by his Spirit we *do* witness the miraculous and see God work in amazing ways. Jesus might have suggested any number of good and godly attributes for us to lift as our highest banner, but instead, he commanded that love be the thing that distinguishes us from everyone else. You may search, but you will not find another world view, religion, or belief system that teaches love in all circumstances. Christianity is unique.

The Apostle John, who was there on the night of Jesus' "Love one another" exhortation would later write, "Beloved, let us love one another, for love is from God, and whoever loves has been born of God and knows God" (I John 4:7). When we love one another, John says, we have been born of God. When we love one another, we bear evidence that we have been loved greatly. When we love one another, others know that we are Christ-followers. Love is what defines us.

Third, and finally, we are to love one another because it's the most evangelistic thing we can do. When Jesus said, "[B]y this will all men know," (John 13:35) there is a bit of irony in his statement. While we worry about strategies for sharing the gospel, and ways to spread the gospel and expand its worldwide influence, the best idea is just to follow Jesus' instructions and live out the gospel in front of a watching world. The gospel in a word is *love*. Maybe as we love one another, our love-starved culture will see us and want what we have.

So, LEO. It may not win football games, but it might just win the world.

DAY THIRTY-ONE

Stir up one another

"And let us consider how to stir up one another to love and good deeds" (Hebrews 10:24).

C.S. Lewis and J.R.R. Tolkien were friends and colleagues who were both professors of English at Oxford University in Great Britain from roughly 1925-1954. Their relationship was a complex one and included some friction over literary approaches and Lewis' choice of the Anglican church instead of the Catholic faith. But for nearly 30 years, these two writers enjoyed a warm camaraderie based on their love of writing. They met every Tuesday morning with four lesser-known literary enthusiasts at an Oxford tavern named The Eagle and the Child in a group they called The Inklings.

During their lifetimes, C.S. Lewis became the more famous of the two men with his plain-spoken defense of the Christian faith through his preaching and a weekly radio show that brought him worldwide attention during World War II. In 1950, the first book of Lewis' classic *Chronicles of Narnia* series called *The Lion, The Witch, and The Wardrobe* was published. We can't be certain, but many have posited that this event lit the fire under J.R.R. Tolkien to want to outdo his literary friend. He had already written *The Hobbit* in 1937, but four years after Lewis' Narnia books started being released, he published *The Lord of The Rings*.

Is this a history and English lesson or a Bible teaching? It's both, I guess. My point is that these two men made each other better authors by sharing ideas, storytelling techniques, and countless manuscripts. When one wrote something clever, the other tried to match it. When the fantasy world of Narnia was created by Lewis, it prompted the Middle Earth of

Tolkien. When Lewis found success in publication and sales, Tolkien tried to best him. It is quite possible that we have two of the greatest classic English book series because these two men pushed each other, or, as the writer of Hebrews would say, they "stirred up" one another. What if this kind of challenging relationship took place in the spiritual realm?

I believe this is exactly what the writer of Hebrews was talking about when he encouraged first-century Christians to "…stir up one another to love and good deeds." Part of the function of community in the Christ-following, *on purpose* life is to push each other to greater levels of living out our faith. The word translated as "stir up" in the English Standard Version of the Bible is far more aggressive than that version makes it sound. This is actually an occasion when the authorized King James Version may be closer to the original meaning. That version says to "provoke" one another to love and good deeds. It refers to the root of the Greek word *paraxusmos* that is literally translated as "sharp" and means "to incite." This is the reaction you would get if you poked someone with a sharp object. In other words, this scripture encourages us to poke sharply or prod each other so that we will love well and do more good deeds!

There is no doubt that we humans need prodding and sharpening from others to make us better. A few years ago, I interviewed some high school basketball coaches from our congregation, and I will never forget what one of them said (my apologies to Coaches Cupples, Mosley, and Witzig for not remembering who actually said it). When I asked why so many people end up in ruts of complacency after graduating from high school, the answer was, "It's because after high school no one coaches us anymore!" Coaches challenge our weaknesses. Coaches make us go farther than we thought we could go. Coaches push us to give our best. Coaches don't let us settle and don't let us quit.

Unfortunately, most of us have no one in our spiritual lives who challenges us to get better, pushes us to try harder, or stretches us further. So… what if we became spiritual coaches for one another in the areas of love and good deeds? This is what the writer of Hebrews says is the role of Christian brothers and sisters within the church. At our best, we stir up one another to increasingly deeper levels of commitment in how we live out our faith. If we are ever going to achieve our highest level of *on purpose* living, others are going to have to challenge, push, and yes, provoke us to it.

It's my prayer that most of you are reading this book with a group of people whom you meet with regularly. It is crucial that you do not try to follow Jesus on your own. The believing life was never meant to be a solo act. If you are not intentionally participating in Christian community, you will probably settle for "good enough." Only as you associate with other brothers and sisters in the faith will you be stirred up to greater and greater love and good deeds. Consider joining a group of like-minded Christ-followers today—your decision will bless you and the kingdom.

For those of us who are in regular community, are you ready to stir? This doesn't have to be an in-your-face experience. Try these three gentle ways of stirring up love and good deeds in those closest to you. 1. Challenge your group to get involved whenever your church organizes an outreach project or a giving emphasis in our community. It only takes one enthusiastic person to get 10-12 people motivated to help those in need. 2. Humbly let others know how God has challenged you to expand your personal serving and loving efforts. As you share what God is doing in your life, you will be spurring others to do the same. 3. Finally, don't hesitate to ask probing questions, in love, of brothers and sisters with whom you have relationships. Share a simple group question like, "When was the last time you felt like you increased your service and love to those around you?" Such an inquiry can be very convicting but also encouraging and can lead to action.

Whenever we can, we want to share real stories with our congregation of those in our fellowship who are loving, giving, and serving as they follow Christ. Many of those we ask are hesitant to record a video or share their testimony on stage. They fear that they will come across as boastful and lacking humility. They prefer to serve without fanfare. But I remind them that if they share how God is inspiring and using them, he will get the glory and everyone else will get the message. So, stir it up.

DAY THIRTY-TWO

Encourage one another

"...not neglecting to meet together, as is the habit of some, but encouraging one another, and all the more as you see the Day drawing near" (Hebrews 10:25)

I was nervously preparing to run my first marathon in Chicago, and as race day approached, I received some strange but valuable advice from a friend who had run the race before. This advice wasn't about hydration, or pace, or breathing, or any of the running tips you might think to give a rookie marathoner. Instead, it was suggested that I write my name somewhere so that people on the sidelines could see it. The day of the race was warm, so I had my wife, Sara, take a magic marker and write "Mike" in large black letters on my bare right arm. As we lined up for the start of the race, I noticed several other runners had done the same thing, so at least I didn't look too weird. I had no idea how valuable this simple tip would be for my ability to complete the race.

Not many miles into the Chicago race, the course winds through Wrigleyville (the neighborhood around Wrigley Field where the Chicago Cubs play baseball), and I discovered why I was told to share my name. The people of Chicago were in their front yards, on their porches, and at the edge of the street to do one thing: encourage the runners. "You look strong, Mike." "Keep going Mike, you can do this." "You got this, Mike." "You're actually running the Chicago Marathon, Mike." "This is going to be your best race ever, Mike." Over and over, comments like these flowed to me from spectators I didn't even know. And closer to the end of the race, I heard, "You're almost there, Mike." "Just a few more miles, Mike." "Wow, you still look really strong, Mike."

How powerful encouragement is when running a race, whether it's the literal Chicago Marathon or the figurative marathon we call life. This is why the verse for today calls Christ-followers to "encourage one another." God knows that living *on purpose* requires lots of encouragement. But what exactly does that mean? Is it just a matter of heaping positive words and ideas on others to make them believe they can do it? Well, that's part of it, but there is far more to encouraging each other.

As is often the case, the Greek word helps us understand exactly what a particular word means. The word translated *encourage* here is the Greek word *parakaleo*. It is essentially a mash up of *para* (beside) and *kaleo* (to call). So to encourage means to call others to your side and put your arm around them (either literally or figuratively) so that they feel your strength and gain renewed courage to take the next step. There are two things to note about encouragement from this verse today.

FIRST: ENCOURAGING IS DONE "IN ASSEMBLY"

Whenever someone asks me whether regular church attendance is biblically important, I point them to this verse. The first century Church met regularly on Sundays in public assemblies just as we do (the word *church* means "called out to assembly") and day by day in their homes (Acts 2:46). The Bible puts a strong emphasis on gathering with other Christ-followers, and it's in this setting that we find great courage to keep going. The year 2020 was a painful illustration of just how discouraging--the opposite of encouraging--our Jesus walk could be when we were unable to gather due to the pandemic.

During those long months, we missed these forms of encouragement and many others--hugs, laughs, smiles, greetings, prayers, public worship, and words of love and affirmation. If you need some encouragement right now, it may be because you have gotten out of the habit of going to church or as the verse says, you "are neglecting to meet together." If you haven't yet come back to our public assembly on Sundays or are still not gathering with a small group during the week, now is the time for you to make that a habit again. You need encouragement and so do those around you. While it's true that we can encourage each other through texts, Zoom calls, and emails, there is nothing like being with real live flesh-and-blood people who cheer you on.

SECOND: ENCOURAGING IS FOR THE FINISH

Another thing to note from this verse is how important encouragement is as we approach the finish line. I was at best a mid-level talent in every sport I played in high school and college. I don't think I had ever before competed in front of more than a couple of hundred spectators—but the Chicago Marathon changed all that. After running 26 miles, I turned the corner and I was greeted by a sea of thousands of spectators cheering from the bleachers that lined the final yards of the course. Here, with the goal in sight and the deafening chorus of encouragement, exhaustion turns into exhilaration. Suddenly, numb legs feel fresh, your breath comes more easily, and many runners actually pick up the pace. Encouragement is powerful through all of the race, but it can carry you across the finish line with a smile on your face.

Encouragement in the church is more and more crucial as we near the finish line. The "Day" mentioned in our verse is none other than the return of Jesus and the beginning of our eternity. This is our spiritual finish line. Here we will experience the roar of the angels' worship, celebrate the presence of God, and rest in Jesus' presence for eternity. But until we cross that line, the running continues. Sometimes the race seems long. Sometimes we feel like quitting. Often, we don't think we have the strength to keep going. The pain in this race of faith is real. But don't give up. Hear the encouragement of the saints: "You can do all things through him who strengthens you." "You are not running alone." "God will finish what he started in you." "You have already won." "Your faith is the victory that overcomes the world."

It almost makes you want to write your name on your arm the next time you go to church, doesn't it?

DAY THIRTY-THREE

Grow up together

"...to equip the saints for the work of ministry, for building up the body of Christ, until we all attain to the unity of the faith and of the knowledge of the Son of God, to mature manhood, to the measure of the stature of the fullness of Christ, so that we may no longer be children, tossed to and fro by the waves and carried about by every wind of doctrine, by human cunning and craftiness in deceitful schemes. Rather, speaking the truth in love, we are to grow up in every way into him who is the head, into Christ, from whom the whole body, joined and held together by every joint with which it is equipped, when each part working properly, makes the body grow so that it builds itself up in love" (Ephesians 4:12-16).

Lines marked carefully, names and dates written in pencil--it's a story of growth. Here are the markings that indicate progress through the years. It is a completely unscientific and yet generally accurate measure of progress towards maturity. In many homes this is the sacred place where parents and grandparents can witness their children growing up right before their eyes. By now, many of you have guessed that I'm talking about the door frame in your home where you record the heights of your kids through the years. If you still don't know what I'm talking about, let me explain one of the greatest low-tech family traditions of all time.

First, the parents (usually mom) start by choosing a doorway that isn't too visible but is located where the family hangs out a lot. Then, as soon as they can toddle over, one by one, the kids are told to stand up straight and tall with their backs against the door frame. Heels have to be flat on the floor, no tippy toes. Then, with great care, mom or dad takes a pencil and marks the door at the top of the child's head with a simple line. After the child steps away, the name of the child and date are recorded next to the line. If there is more than one child, the next sibling steps up and the procedure is repeated--line, name, date. It is the official family record of maturity on that day. At some point (it could be months later, or just a rainy day when everyone is bored), everyone returns to the door frame to be measured again.

For many families, this ritual lasts for most of the children's growing-up years. Kids actually get excited when they see that their new mark on the door frame is higher than the previous one. Why? Because as you're growing, you don't really notice it happening. You can't see it or feel it. But you are growing nonetheless. The line on the door confirms that you are, in fact, changing. If you have two or three children and follow this practice for years, the door frame is filled with progressively higher lines, names, and dates that chronicle the physical growth of your family. This is a snapshot, on a wooden portal, of growing up together. Some people value this memento of progress so much that they remove the frame from the door and take it with them if they move. Wouldn't it be helpful if we had a door frame with marks on it for our spiritual lives?

Today's verses are complex and there is a lot we could unpack here, but it's basically teaching us how we are to measure our growing up together. That phrase "measure of the stature" (Ephesians 4:5) is actually referring to how progress in age or height is measured. In fact, the Greek word for measure is the word *metron,* which is where we get the measurement known as a meter. In these verses, the apostle is encouraging Christians-- then and now--to grow up together and watch for tangible ways to measure growth and maturity. So stand up straight, no tippy toes, and let's see where we are today with the spiritual growth lines the apostle has marked out for us.

The first mark is at the very top of the spiritual door frame. It's the fullness of our big brother, Jesus. It's so high that we may think we'll never measure up. But he is the model of growth that God has planned for us. The goal is maturity (mature manhood), v. 13. In the Greek language, mature is the word *teleios* and literally means "to be complete, full, or finished." No younger sibling looks at the marks on the door frame, and seeing where his older brothers or sisters measure, thinks, "I'm just gonna stay here at this height. I don't want to grow." Instead, noting the heights of our family members makes us want to be as tall as they are. This is the importance of living *on purpose* together. Jesus is our goal, but we have family members of the faith who are more mature, and by noticing their growth, we realize that we no longer want to stay spiritual infants.

The second mark we aspire to on the sacred door frame is the work of ministry for building up the body. Here Paul mixes metaphors of physical growth with the construction terminology of house building. As you stand next to your personal maturity line, ask yourself if you are working to "build up" the body of Jesus. This aspect of maturity is so important. We have been equipped by the Holy Spirit (as we already learned in Day 27) to build up the body of Christ, his Church. If you are working to build up others, you are maturing and becoming taller and taller in your faith. We grow up together as we serve and work for one another.

The third mark on the door frame of faith is unity. Siblings in biological families and in the spiritual family are not supposed to be clones of one another. In fact, the beauty of God's creative diversity is that the church family is made up of people of different races, socio-economic standing, sexes, generations, origins, backgrounds, personalities, and talents. But there is a line in common that we all must measure up to, and that is the line of unity. We may see some things differently, but when it comes to faith and to the knowledge of the Son of God, there is no wiggle room. This is why what we believe about who Jesus is, and what we profess about our source of authoritative teaching (the Bible), must never waiver. We are growing together when we are unified in Jesus.

The fourth and final line that measures our maturity is speaking the truth in love. Paul says here that "speaking the truth in love, we are to grow up in him in every way." A sure sign of a "growing up together" community is that we are able to speak the truth in love to one another. "Grace and truth came through Jesus Christ" (John 1:17). His balance is the line we are growing toward. As you stand next to the line that is grace *and* truth, you may prefer one or the other. Some of us speak words that are gracious, but they're not fully truthful. Others easily blurt out the truth (which we sometimes call "being authentic") but do it in a way that is hurtful to others. In the church, as we grow together, we mature to the point that we can speak and hear words that are true because we are confident that the person sharing them has our very best interests in mind.

So how tall are you in your Christian maturity? Where do you need to grow? How tall do you want to be? Remember that spiritually speaking we are standing with our backs to the door frame. We rarely feel growth or see it as it happens. So let this chapter be one measurement line in your growth journey. Next time, I'm sure your mark on the spiritual wall will be higher because by God's grace he is growing us, and by his design we are growing together.

DAY THIRTY-FOUR

Work together

"I entreat Euodia and Syntyche to agree in the Lord. Yes, I ask you also, true companion, help these women, who have labored side by side with me the gospel together with Clement and the rest of my fellow workers, whose names are written in the book of life" *(Philippians 4:2&3).*

It happened during one of my earlier visits to India. The leadership team from our church, my wife, and I were taking in the sights and sounds of that country's incredible culture. We had come to teach, preach, and encourage the Christians there, and we were hosted by our good friends, Ajai and Indu Lall, in a rural town (of 2 million!) called Damoh. We witnessed many different ways that they were serving their community--operating a hospital, a nursing and evangelism schools, and a children's home. But we were not prepared for Ajai's announcement to the group one morning that after breakfast we would be going to feed the widows. We willingly followed him to the designated location, but we had no idea what to expect.

We arrived, and as we came around the corner of a building, there under a makeshift tent we encountered a kaleidoscope of colors. Hundreds of women, dressed in their vibrant traditional saris, were sitting on the ground. All age groups were represented among these widowed women who now were left with no source of income. Although they received a government subsidy of about $2 a month, they were living in poverty. We had come to encourage them and to distribute a 20-pound bag of rice and a new sari to each woman. After a word of encouragement from my wife Sara, we distributed the rice and clothing. I look back on this as one of my very favorite ministry experiences.

I was profoundly moved by the deep appreciation these dear women showed; their smiles communicated what they could not say in English. But I was also blessed by one of those "frozen in time" moments where I took in a ministry scene that seemed to unfold in slow motion. To my right, I saw my wife Sara kissing an older woman on the face. In front of me, one of our pastors was kneeling and holding the hands of a widow. Two other co-workers were bent over, delivering bags of rice to the women in front of them. Everywhere I turned, I saw beautiful scenes of servanthood. Here we were, side by side, serving in the name of the Lord. This is a picture of life together *on purpose*. We are fellow workers in the kingdom.

The word used for "fellow workers" in this passage is that word *sunergos* (synergy), a word we looked at when we began this section of our journey. What I love about these verses is that we actually get to hear about some of our first century Christian brothers and sisters from the church in Philippi. It is humbling to realize that we are part of something that started 2,000 years ago with real people like you and me. They were working together then for the same faith that we share—all these years later. Let's meet these ancient Christ-followers and learn from them about working together.

Paul begins by mentioning Euodia and Syntyche, two women whom he had worked with and who were obviously leaders in the church. While we're not sure exactly what the issue was between these two women, we acknowledge that Christians don't always agree on how our faith is to be lived out personally and in the church. When we are engaged in ministry, there are often several biblically acceptable ways to serve and do the work of the gospel. Maybe Euodia wanted to focus on orphans and widows and Syntyche thought they should be training people to share their faith instead. What they disagreed on is not important. Paul's point is that disagreements should never lead to division among fellow workers. Agreeing to do the work someone else's way or finding a compromise between various approaches is more important than having your own way. Who do you need to "agree with in the Lord"?

The next name we come across does not seem to be an actual name in most translations. You might have noticed that in verse 3 Paul addressed a "true companion" (in this translation), but that phrase has also been translated "loyal yoke fellow." Who was this? It must have been someone that the entire congregation would have known because these letters were commonly read in community. This is why most scholars believe that this is a man whose given name is *Syzygos* (Greek word for yokefellow). In this case, verse three would read, "I ask you, loyal Syzygos, to help these women who have labored side by side with me...". It's quite possible that Syzygos was one of the overseers (elders) who Paul addressed at the beginning of this letter (Philippians 1:1). In any case, we are encouraged to be like Syzygos and to help servants in the church work well together.

Finally, we are introduced to Clement, another member of this ancient congregation at Philippi. He is associated with those who are fellow workers and those who have "labored side by side with me in the gospel." Here, Paul actually uses a first century athletic term for striving together in competition (the Greek word is *sunathleo* which has our word athlete in it). It would be like us saying, "Let's do this!" This is our encouragement to work graciously together toward the same goal as we follow Jesus. And that goal is to advance the good news of our salvation to everyone as we grow in our faith.

Whatever we feel God is calling us to, he is calling us to do it with others. When we put aside our personal wants, focus on the work, and strive toward the same goal, we are at our Christ-following best. Like these early Christians, this isn't always easy, and we're not perfect in the execution. But as we work in community, we are assured that our names are written in the book of life alongside Euodia, Syntyche, Syzygos, and Clement. And that is something worth working for... together.

DAY THIRTY-FIVE

I am with you always

"And Jesus came and said to them, 'All authority in heaven and on earth has been given to me. Go therefore and make disciples of all nations, baptizing them in the name of the Father and of the Son and of the Holy Spirit, teaching them to observe all that I have commanded you. And behold, I am with you always, to the end of the age'" (Matthew 28:18-20).

We began this week standing with Moses on the mountain as he asked God if he could just send someone else to do the work God was calling him to. And indeed, God did send someone **with** Moses and is also sending others **with us** as we live *on purpose*. It is only in this community of loving one another, stirring up one another, building up one another, and working with one another that we can truly live out our calling for God. But make no mistake… the work that he is sending us into is far bigger than we could ever imagine being able to accomplish. Yet still he sends. Just as God said to Moses, "Now therefore, go…," he is telling us to "go" into the purpose he has for us. Just as God sent Moses into Egypt to free the Hebrew people from bondage, he is sending us into the world to make disciples. But he is not just sending us with each other—he's coming with us.

The Scripture at the beginning of today's chapter is commonly referred to as The Great Commission. If you think the Lord's calling was immense for Moses, it pales in comparison to the vast scope of this calling. No matter what we have discovered about our purpose in this world, it is clear that God is calling all of us to go into the whole world and make disciples.

129

In a minute, I'll explain exactly what Jesus is sending us into, but most of this chapter is written to encourage us to move forward with confidence, knowing that he is with us. So, what is this great commissioning that God is giving us?

Many people want to accentuate the baptism that Jesus orders for new believers, or highlight the importance of teaching, or focus on the missional emphasis of going. These things are all significant, but none of these are the main thrust of Jesus' desire for us in his final earthly instructions. The point of these verses is that disciples make disciples. A disciple literally means "learner" or "pupil" and is another word for follower. This describes the first century practice of learning by following a teacher (rabbi). Students didn't sit in classrooms in Jesus' day; they followed and learned as they watched, listened to, and had dialogue with their rabbi.

The Great Commission, then, is a call for those of us who are already disciples of Jesus to invite others to follow him too. This is much more organic than most of us think. The "go" part of this verse literally means, "as you are going." So to "go" is not so much a call to "go on a mission trip" (even though that can be valuable) as it is to "go through your everyday life" seeing your part of the world as a mission field. This is where your *on purpose* call and Jesus' commission come together. As you live out Jesus' specific calling for your life at school, at home, at the gym, at the grocery store, at work, in your neighborhood, or in your social circles, make disciples. The great commission is this simple: Live your Christ-following life in a loving and winsome way everywhere you go and invite as many as you can to find what you have found. And before you begin to make excuses, as I am often tempted to do, and as Moses did and as anyone else who's ever followed God has, let me tell you why Jesus thinks we can fulfill this commission.

We can fulfill this commission because all authority on heaven and earth has been given to Jesus. Remember Jesus' timing on giving this speech to his first century followers? It was **after** his death, burial, and resurrection! Who has authority over death? Jesus. Who has authority over sin? Jesus. Who has authority over Satan? Jesus. "Therefore, God has exalted him and bestowed on him the name that is above every other name, so that at the name of Jesus every knee should bow, in heaven and on earth and under the earth, and every tongue confess that Jesus Christ is Lord, to the glory of God the Father" (Philippians 2:9&10). We are not inviting people to follow Jesus on our own authority (or ability, gifting, or calling for that matter). It is the authority of Jesus that allows us to be bold enough to make disciples as we go. But there's more.

We can fulfill the commission because Jesus says, "I am with you always." If he sent us out by ourselves to make disciples, it would still be a great (though highly improbable) commissioning. If he sent us out with just one another (as we have discussed this week), it would still be a great (and at least less lonely) commissioning. But he sends us with each other *and with his presence*, the indwelling Holy Spirit. Here is what we need to know as we get ready to head into our Egypt. Here is what we need to hold onto as we live out who we are in Christ. Here is the only confidence we can really have in our calling. Jesus is with us.

We can live *on purpose* because the one who has a purpose for us will be there with us. Be encouraged by these additional scriptures: "If God is for us, who can be against us?" (Romans 8:31) and "...he has said, 'I will never leave you nor forsake you'" (Hebrews 13:5).

CAN SOMEONE ELSE GO?
EXODUS 4:13-17

Days 29-35

Even after learning our spiritual gifts, knowing who we are in Jesus, becoming confident in who God is, and identifying areas where we can be more intentional in our lives, we still often hesitate to live out our calling. Maybe we, like Moses in Exodus 4, don't want to follow God's purpose for us because we are afraid, lack in faith, or are just complacent and comfortable. Whatever the hesitancy is for each of us, the antidote is believing that God is with us and that he provides others to walk side by side with us. Living on purpose is a team sport and is most successfully done with the help and encouragement of other people. In our work for him, God provides sisters and brothers to be our spiritual companions.

Let's get started. . .

1. What stands out from Sunday's sermon and helps you understand this week's theme? Take a moment and review the Day Twenty-Nine reading. What do you note that helps you remember this week's question?

2. Watch the "Can Someone Else Go?" teaching video. Reflect on it and discuss your thoughts.

3. This week's devotions focus on five specific ways a community of believers supports one another. You may want to highlight all

five or choose just one of the devotions to focus on to answer the following:

- Of the five ways (Love, stir up, encourage, grow, work) which have had the most impact in your life of serving with others?

- Of these, which do you need the most right now? Which are you most likely to share?

- Take some time and talk through how your group can live these out with one another.

4. Just as God promised to be with Moses. Jesus promises he will be with you and me. How does the Day Thirty-Five devotional encourage you as you think about how you are called to live intentionally and within God's purpose for your life?

5. Keep in mind that one of the beautiful "on purpose" plans of God is that your group, together, embodies multiple spiritual gifts. When your group is functioning well in using all of its member's gifts, it is designed to be a mini-church that brings life and light to your community.

6. Based upon your group's gifts, identify people and places that your group could focus on serving and helping. Take time to identify an individual, a family, or group of people that your group can serve in specific ways. For example, consider a particular school, a sports team, or a location in your community that could be blessed by your group.

7. Read Exodus 4:13-17. God provided Aaron as a spiritual companion in Moses' journey. God can do the same for you and me. Take a moment and write down 2 or 3 names of fellow believers who could encourage you to live on purpose.

8. Now that you've identified a couple of people, where are the places you could serve together as you are called to live on purpose? Are you willing to have these friends to pray for you and hold you accountable as they encourage and work with you?

Ok, so now what. . .

Final Takeaway. . . What is one specific way you will live on purpose this week?

_____

_____

_____

Next Steps. . .

- Contact the 2-3 people you identified. Invite them to journey with you in prayer, service, encouragement, and accountability for the next month, and perhaps beyond. Share how God has been guiding you through this study and showing you your gifts.

- Keep completing your daily reading.

For Further Reflection. . .

- Spend some time with the resources located in the Appendix for Week 5.

- There are a number of written resources that explain how a smaller group of people can commit to sharing their lives and encouraging one another. We suggest that you to read any of the following:

  - *Sacred Companionship* - David Benner

  - *Transforming Discipleship* - Greg Ogden

DAY THIRTY-SIX

Can I Go In Peace?

"Moses went back to Jethro his father-in-law and said to him, 'Please let me go back to my brothers in Egypt to see whether they are still alive.' And Jethro said to Moses, 'Go in peace.' And the Lord said to Moses in Midian, 'Go back to Egypt, for all the men who were seeking your life are dead.' So Moses took his wife and his sons and had them ride a donkey, and back to the land of Egypt. And Moses took the staff of God in his hand." Exodus 4:18-20

On the mountaintops, your vision expands, and the big picture is clearer. Your perspective changes. High in the peaks, your mind and soul ascend with the elevation. Here, you leave behind the daily monotony and catch a glimpse of God's eternal purpose. It is in these majestic locations that reflection, breathing deeply, and taking inventory seem to occur naturally. There's a reason that the best times in our lives are called mountaintop experiences. But as wonderful as the mountains may be (both physically and spiritually), living out God's purpose for our lives takes place mostly in the valleys.

By Exodus 4, a lot has changed for Moses since he first turned aside to see the mysterious burning bush on Horeb, the mountain of God. He has learned a lot about himself and about the God of his forefathers. The *all-existent* God has revealed his purpose for this former prince of Egypt turned shepherd. Moses has taken inventory of where he is, who he is (and is not), and how God intends to use him to deliver the Israelites from the bondage of slavery in Egypt. God has equipped him with his staff and his presence. God has answered every concern, reassured him through every fear, and been patient in his unwillingness. Their conversation truly has been a *holy ground* experience; but as holy as the ground may have been, Moses cannot live out his purpose on the mountain. He has to go, but there is still one question remaining.

Prayerfully, the mountain of this forty-day study has caused us to experience much of what Moses experienced 3,500 years ago. We have considered five questions from Exodus 3 and 4 along with this man of God. We have come to a better understanding of who we are, who God is, and what God intends to do through us. We have reflected on the running and wandering aspects of our lives and we are now ready to follow. With Moses, we have experienced *holy ground* moments and have discovered the presence and power of Jesus in our lives. And now, like our ancient brother, we are called to take the first steps of living *on purpose*. We must go. And like him, there is one question we still need to have answered.

CAN I GO IN PEACE?

Moses now has a clear vision and purpose for his future, yet he does not set out for Egypt directly from the mountain. First, he must be reunited with his family members who live in Midian, which may be as far 120 miles from where he met with God. As he made the two to three week journey home, he must have rehearsed what he would say to his wife, his sons, and his father-in-law. Once there, he would try to communicate all that had transpired, explain God's new plan for his life, and perhaps most importantly, seek affirmation from those he loved and trusted the most.

Remember that Moses was now eighty years old and was almost certainly seen as wise in the ancient eastern culture in which he lived. And yet, when he returned to Midian, he sought the blessing of someone older and wiser. He essentially asked for permission to carry out his mission in Egypt. "Please let me go back..." he said to his father-in-law in Exodus 4:18. This conversation was an important final step in moving forward with his calling. He needed to come to a place of peace by being affirmed by those closest to him. There are three specific steps Moses models as he moves into this final phase of life *on purpose*.

Day Thirty-Six

SEEK SPIRITUAL, TRUSTED INPUT

By asking for Jethro's permission, Moses is displaying godly humility and submission. As we said earlier, rarely is one called to do something for God alone. God has given us people in our lives who either have authority over us or are older, wiser, and/or more mature in their faith. Though we have noted that Jethro's priesthood was not the pure faith in the covenant God of Abraham (for example, they obviously didn't practice circumcision), he was still someone who had spiritual wisdom. Moses humbles himself and submits himself to another trusted voice. What would have happened if Jethro had denied his request? We'll never know. What we do know is that his affirmation gave Moses the confidence that someone else felt that his return to Egypt was a sound plan. Our individual gifts and calling in the church function in much the same way.

The first step I challenge you to take in any endeavor is to seek godly input from other Christ-followers. These may be the people in your small group who are following Jesus with you, or it could be a mentor, pastor, or trusted church member whom you can trust. Whether you're considering selling your house, leaving your job and moving to foreign country, or thinking about teaching a kids' class at church, talk to Christian brothers or sisters. Let them ask questions and make comments and then seek their blessing for your next steps. If they are hesitant, it doesn't mean that you have missed your calling. Just slow down. In most instances, the input you get from other believers will enhance your *on purpose* life and they will give you their blessing.

SEEK PEACE

Here is what Jethro does for Moses: He gives a simple three-word blessing for Moses to follow God's call. He says, "Go in peace." You probably know the Hebrew word for peace is the word *shalom*. This was (and is) a greeting and a blessing—really a prayer of sorts that asks God to give you a settled soul, contentment, and confidence in your life. The signs were clear that Moses was to go and lead the people of God to freedom, but this blessing of Jethro's was the peace he sought. Peace is not just an

Old Testament blessing; it is part of the Christ-following *on purpose* life for us as well.

How do we find peace aside from the affirmation of another trusted, spiritual Christian? The Holy Spirit is at work in all believers, all the time, to produce this fruit in us (Galatians 5:22). A simple way to have peace is to pray "Holy Spirit, give me peace as I take these steps of faith in my calling." Another way to seek peace in your purpose and calling is to note whether or not you find joy in your decision. When you consider using your gifts in a specific way for God's kingdom, do you feel joyful? Finally, kingdom impact will give you peace. You will notice that using your gift is making a difference in the lives of those around you. Every calling, gifting, and purpose for a believer is for the benefit of others. There are no self-serving gifts. As you serve others and see your influence for Jesus increase in the lives of those around you, you can have peace that you are in the right place.

TAKE A SMALL, FIRST STEP OF OBEDIENCE AND FAITH

It may seem like an unimportant detail to the overall story, but I believe Moses' actions in Exodus 4:20 are a significant lesson for us. Following God is a journey that is lived out one step at a time. There are so many details that Moses still didn't have about how he would lead God's people out of Egypt. Yet he did what he knew he was to do that day. He packed up his family for a long journey, took the staff of God in his hand, and "went back to the land of Egypt" (Exodus 4:20). Do you know how you make a 200 mile journey across the desert to the land of Egypt? You take one step at a time, beginning with the first step. Life *on purpose* means following God through steps of faith and obedience day by day.

After thirty-six days of discovering and affirming our purpose in Jesus Christ together, it's now time for your first steps in this journey. As you discover how God has made and gifted you as you follow Christ, what tangible action can you take to live *on purpose*? Don't let this study end as just a spiritual, feel-good, mountaintop experience. Do something with what you have discovered. Spend time this week writing on the page provided at the end of this section. Write your plan for following God in the area of your calling. How do you need to rearrange your life to live your purpose? Write it down. What measurable way(s) can you live out your purpose in the next month? Write it down. What long-term expressions of your purpose may be possible through the Holy Spirit? Dream a little and write it down.

We finish this book with four blessings for the journey. Each of the next four days, read them as you pray about and move into the calling God has revealed for your life. We are no longer running from our past or from our boredom. We are no longer wandering aimlessly through life and wondering what it's all about. We are following Jesus because we have found our purpose in him. Now it's time to go. Go in peace.

DAY THIRTY-SEVEN

Blessing of love

"Now may our God and Father himself, and our Lord Jesus, direct our way to you, and may the Lord make you increase and abound in love for one another and for all, as we do for you, so that he may establish your hearts blameless in holiness before our God and Father, at the coming of our Lord Jesus with all his saints" (I Thessalonians 3:11-13)

Spiritually speaking, blessing someone is a much bigger action than we imagine. We tend to throw the word *blessing* around in a haphazard "good luck" way without really grasping the significance of that word. For example, we respond, "Bless you" when someone sneezes. Or we see helpless or hapless people and say, "God bless them." Sometimes Christians will use "God bless" as a farewell at the end of a letter or email (I've done this myself many times). But a blessing is more than this.

A blessing is a word of favor or goodness from someone of great power or position over a person less powerful. The word itself means "to kneel or bow," so it is proper to kneel before someone greater and receive a word of blessing. Most often in the Bible, it is God who gives the blessing. Only God can truly bless. However, from Scripture we learn that one person can invoke God's goodness upon someone else in a way that becomes reality. Sometimes, our blessing of others is verbalizing a prayer over them to indicate what we believe God is going to do in their lives. So when Jethro said, "Go in peace" to Moses, by faith this was a prayer of blessing given for his journey.

The Bible is full of these kinds of blessing-prayers, and just as in the end Moses received blessing for his calling, it is appropriate that we end our *on purpose* journey together with four prayers. Two of these prayers are from the pen of the apostle Paul to churches he loved; one prayer is more intimate and directed to a good friend of Paul's; the final prayer was given by God for the high priest Aaron to pronounce over the Hebrew people.

Our verses for today are from Paul's first letter to the church in the northern Greek city of Thessalonica (today called Thessaloniki—I have the Starbucks mug to prove it!). Remember that it was in this city that Paul's sermons caused a riot, led to some arrests, and that eventually led to Paul leaving secretly, by night (Acts 17:1-10). In this Scripture passage, he writes to the Christ-followers there and he prays over them (and us) a beautiful blessing/prayer. As you read the rest of this chapter, take a posture of receiving this blessing. If you can, lift your palms heavenward and be blessed by these ancient Spirit-inspired words.

MAY THE LORD BLESS YOU WITH DIRECTION FOR YOUR WAY

Paul begins by praying that the Thessalonica Christians would be led by God the Father and Christ his son. In the Jesus-following way, going his direction is as simple as walking in his will and as complex as knowing where to live, what career to pursue, which person to date, or what school to attend. The biblical guidelines for being a Christ-follower are clear, but the daily specifics sometimes are not. So, as each of us pursues his or her purpose, may God direct each one of us in the details.

MAY THE LORD MAKE YOU INCREASE AND ABOUND IN LOVE

The blessing continues, speaking about the love that we have for one another. Notice the reciprocal nature of this love prayer. We learned on day 30 of our *on purpose* journey that as we discover our calling, it is nurtured in an environment of love and it continues to grow. The apostle is praying first that our love for one another and all people will increase. But this prayer goes on to assure us that we will receive an increasing love in return, as noted when he writes "…as we do for you." We are truly blessed when we find our purpose in a community where love is given and received in increasing measure. In this setting, God's love for us is celebrated, our love for others is encouraged, and the love we receive is the natural outcome.

MAY THE LORD ESTABLISH YOUR HEARTS BLAMELESS IN HOLINESS

Finally, Paul prays words of blessing for our future. Remember that these are words of favor from God as we kneel before him. This is a prayer that will be realized in Jesus. You and I will have hearts that are blameless in holiness. As you receive this part of the blessing, you may wonder how it is possible that the imperfect people you know (especially the person you see in the mirror everyday) could ever be blessed with blameless and holy hearts. The short answer is Jesus; the long answer is that it's a process.

The word *blameless* here means literally "not finding fault" and *holiness* means "set apart." So how can we ever have a heart that no one can find fault with? The only way is Jesus making it so. His blood has washed away the faults and blame of our hearts through his death, burial, and resurrection. Incredibly, the Bible says that Jesus is our defense lawyer (I John 2:1) who testifies before God that we are without sin. This is our eternal, spiritual reality. But what about the not-so-blameless aspects of our hearts that surface from time to time? As we follow Jesus by faith and seek to live out his purpose for us, he is making us new day by day. We are not finished yet, but God promises that he will finish what he started in us.

These are today's *on purpose* prayers. Thank God for blessing you with the guidance of his Spirit. Thank God for the love you receive and have the strength to give to others. Thank God for his work in your heart that will be completed in holiness. If you have these three things today, you are blessed. Go in peace.

DAY THIRTY-EIGHT

Blessing on sharing our faith

"I thank my God always when I remember you in my prayers, because I hear of your love and of the faith that you have toward the Lord Jesus and for all the saints. And I pray that the sharing of your faith may become effective for the full knowledge of every good thing that is in us for the sake of Christ. For I have derived much joy and comfort from your love, my brother, because of the hearts of the saints have been refreshed through you" (Philemon 4-7).

What an incredible treasure we have in this short personal letter penned by the apostle Paul in the first century to his friend and brother in Christ, Philemon. The Holy Spirit has preserved Paul's epistles and personal letters for us. Most of them, like Ephesians or Philippians, are theologically heavy and contain his teachings on how to lead the Jesus-following life and live as Christians. But the book that we take our lesson from today is among Paul's letters that specifically address individuals. Some of these letters focus on instruction in ministry and church leadership, as is the case with Paul's letters to Timothy and Titus. In each of these, there are declarations of Christian love, friendship, and genuine concern, but somehow, Philemon feels different. There is an intimacy in this letter that displays the genuine friendship that Paul shared with this Christian brother.

Who was this man that Paul was so attached to, and what is the story behind the letter? A quick look at some of Paul's other letters helps us piece the puzzle together. Historically, we understand that Philemon was a house group leader in the church at Colossae. Although Paul doesn't confirm this, the names mentioned in this letter were listed as members of the Colossian fellowship. Archippus is mentioned in verse one of Philemon and in Colossians 4:17, as is a man by the name of Onesimus. Paul writes to Philemon regarding Onesimus, saying in chapter 12, "I am sending him back to you" and, "I have sent… Onesimus, our faithful and beloved brother, who is one of you." These clues seem to confirm that Paul sent this letter to Philemon via Tychicus who also carried the letter that we now know as Colossians (see Colossians 4:7). This is the background for this letter, the biblical book of Philemon. And one more thing: Paul is writing to Philemon from Rome… where he is in prison.

Although we are not given all of the details, it appears that while he was imprisoned in Rome Paul met Onesimus, apparently a former servant of Philemon, who had run away (Philemon 16). We can't verify this sequence biblically, but a captured runaway slave would have been imprisoned and returned to his former owner. Perhaps Onesimus was thrown into the cell next to Paul who recognized him from his time in Colossae.

I'd like to think that Paul, the evangelist, opened a conversation with the prisoner Onesimus and they discovered that they both knew Philemon. Maybe Paul either converted him to Christianity in that Roman prison or had done so earlier at the church in Colossae. While we do not know every detail, we do know that Paul became quite attached to Onesimus as shown by the following lines: "I appeal to you for my child, Onesimus, whose father I became in my imprisonment" (Philemon 10) and "I am sending him back to you, sending my very heart" (Philemon 12). So how can we read this letter as a blessing for *on purpose* living in the 21st century? There are at least three things to consider.

READ PHILEMON AS A BLESSING TO REFRESH OTHERS WITH A SINCERE FAITH

When Paul says that he has "heard about his [Philemon's] love and faith toward Jesus and for all the saints," Paul is repeating someone's description of Philemon. The remarkable aspect of this assessment of Philemon's life is that it probably came from his former servant, Onesimus. Think about it logically. The one person who had an intimate relationship with

Philemon would have been his house servant, Onesimus. He would have seen him under the stress of business, in his private time, and when the church gathered in his home. And this servant, who could have been bitter or vindictive under the pressure of servanthood, actually testified that Philemon was a true man of faith. May we live *on purpose* like Philemon so that everyone in our lives can be refreshed by our sincere faith.

READ PHILEMON AS A BLESSING FOR APPEALING TO OTHERS INSTEAD OF DEMANDING FROM OTHERS

Another blessed part of this prayer is found in Paul's appeal for Philemon to grant Onesimus his freedom so that he might become a partner in his ministry. It appears that Paul believed that he would have been justified in demanding that Philemon release his servant to Paul ("to say nothing of your owing me even your own self" v. 19b), but instead he left room for Philemon to act out his faith by his own choice. Sometimes we Christ-followers tend to demand that others take the same steps that we are taking on the journey of faith. Instead, we should patiently allow room for God to work in their lives. May we live *on purpose* like Paul in ways that hope and pray for the best in others and give them room to grow.

READ PHILEMON AS A BLESSING FOR BROTHERHOOD FOR ALL

There is one final lesson in this biblical letter to our ancient brother in Christ. I am very aware that we live in a culture that is still reeling from the evils of our history of slavery and that this letter deals with a servant and master from the first century. Slavery as it existed in our history is never condoned in the Bible, and here Paul appeals to something greater than civic reform. He appeals instead to the equality and brotherhood that can be found only in the church. Within the church, there is no hierarchy of master and servant because we are all servants of Jesus. May we live *on purpose* in such a way that we always consider others to be as important and valuable as we are.

On Purpose

Unfortunately, we don't have Philemon's response to Paul's letter, but given Philemon's sincere love and faith, we may assume that he refreshed Paul and Onesimus by releasing his servant to work for Christ with Paul. May you and I be as refreshing as Philemon as we live *on purpose*.

DAY THIRTY-NINE

Blessing for far more

"Now to him who is able to do far more abundantly that all that we ask for think, according to the power at work within us, to him be the glory in the church and in Christ Jesus throughout all generations, forever and ever. Amen" (Ephesians 3:20&21).

We prayed, "Lord, increase our impact for your kingdom through our online campus," thinking that an increase of a thousand viewers each year would be amazing. An Eastview couple prayed, "Lord, help us facilitate the building of homes for people in Haiti," thinking that they would travel to Haiti a couple of times a year to do that. Eastview leaders prayed, "Lord, give us the resources to rebuild what the government destroyed in the slums of Nairobi," and we hoped that our church family could raise $40,000 to contribute. Our church prayed, "God, help us love and serve our community more than we ever have," as we brainstormed ways to expand our food pantry. I personally prayed an immature but filled-with-faith prayer in my preteen years: "Lord, allow me to preach in a big church," while imagining a church of 500-600 attendees. What are you asking God for?

Now that we have some idea of what it means to live *on purpose* for Jesus, what are you thinking that God might do with you next? What do you envision him accomplishing by using the Holy Spirit gifts he has empowered you with as you work for the kingdom? How do you think God will use your weaknesses and abilities in the church where you belong? What could God do through the group of people you do life with as you take the next steps of faith together? What is the greatest spiritual victory you can imagine? If you stretch your mind to the extreme, where might God take you in the next five years? Go ahead. Take a few minutes right now. Think. Pray. Dream. Imagine. Wonder.

Here's what I know about whatever you or I picture that God might accomplish in us and through us: It's not big enough. How do I know? Because the verse above is a blessing for God to do far more in our lives than we can imagine. I also know it because that is the testimony of a long line of men and women of faith. When we are following God, he does far more than we can ask for or imagine. It was true for Isaiah in the Old Testament. In Isaiah 49, the prophet declared how honored he was that the Lord had used him to lead the nation of Israel back to God. But God gives a "more" response: "It is too light [small] a thing that you should be my servant to raise up the tribes of Jacob... I will make you as a light for the nations, that my salvation may reach to the ends of the earth" (Isaiah 49:6). Isaiah's prayer was, "Lord use me as your mouthpiece," while he hoped to call Israel to repentance. But God had him prophesy about Jesus, the one who would bring salvation to all humanity. Our prayers are often too small, while God's answers are often much bigger and far more.

As we pay one last visit to Moses, mentioned so often in our study, we see that this prayer-of-asking pattern played out in ever-increasing frequency over his lifetime. Moses was born under Pharaoh's edict that all baby boys born to Hebrew parents should be thrown into the Nile. But when Moses was born, his parents prayed, "Lord, spare our son's life," hoping he would live to be a slave. When Moses fled from Pharaoh after committing murder, he prayed, "Lord spare my life," thinking he could start over far from Egypt. And God answered both of these prayers by doing more. "Spare our son's life" and "Spare my life" turned into God sparing the Hebrew nation through Moses. God is like that. I've seen "more" answers thousands of times in my life and ministry.

Let's go back to the prayers I mentioned at the beginning of this chapter. In the fall of 2019 when our church prayed for God to increase our kingdom impact through our online campus, we believed we could have 10,000 weekly viewers by 2025. But when the Covid pandemic shut down our church for four months, we averaged over 15,000 viewers weekly and 25,000+ on Easter! When Steve and Shelly Hari first prayed about building homes in Haiti, they didn't know that God would have them move there full-time to start a ministry that has built over a hundred homes. When our church prayed to raise $40,000 to rebuild with our brother Pastor Shadrack in Kenya, God blew up that number and our church family gave $250,000 instead. Those gifts expanded the influence of our Kenyan mission field exponentially. Again, when we prayed for God to help us influence our local community, we were not expecting him to provide a very reasonably-priced church building in the perfect location that would become our community center.

This brings me to my personal journey. As I share, I ask for your forgiveness if this comes across as anything but giving all the glory to God for what he has allowed me to be part of here at Eastview. I can't express how little I had to do with all of it. Here's what I know. Unlike most people, I had a very clear sense of God's calling on my life by the age of six. He created me to be a preacher. The clarity of understanding that I've had is what I'm praying that God has revealed to you during this *on purpose* journey. There is nothing that will simplify every decision in life like knowing the purpose God has for you. The reality is this: It is easier to live *on purpose* when you know your purpose.

Back to my story. In my preteen years, I started praying that God would let me preach in a large church someday. I had grown up in churches of average size, which meant less than 100 attendees on Sundays (the average church in America has about 70 people in weekly attendance, at least before Covid). But when I was in the 4th grade, we moved to a church that grew to about 500 people. I thought it was amazing to see everything God could do with that many people. So, because I already knew God's call on my life, I prayed nightly, for four or five years, that God would allow me to preach in an equally big church one day. Later, as a teen, I stopped praying that "big church" prayer because I realized that I would be willing to preach in any size church.

So what does God do with the sincere prayers of a kid whose childlike faith leads him to pray that he might preach in a church of 500 people? He could have laughed and said, "You can't do it, son." Or he could have said, "How presumptuous of you; what a selfish request." How did God answer everything that I was able to ask or imagine as a 10-year old? In my case, he did far more. He took my weaknesses, my faults and failures, and surrounded me with countless mentors to encourage me and help me grow in my preaching. Now he lets me preach in a church of thousands every week. I'm amazed every time I preach. The glory is his!

So what are you asking and imagining that God might do in your life? I'd encourage you, by faith, to ask for more… and then be ready for God to do far more even than that!

DAY FORTY

Priestly blessing

"The Lord spoke to Moses, saying, 'Speak to Aaron and his sons, saying, thus you shall bless the people of Israel: you shall say to them, 'The Lord bless you and keep you; the Lord make his face to shine upon you and be gracious to you; the Lord lift up his countenance upon you and give you peace.' So shall they put my name upon the people of Israel, and I will bless them." *(Numbers 6:22-27).*

Although I was sitting on a sunny beach in California, my soul was partly cloudy and cool with a chance of rain. Without being overly transparent or dramatic, I had some concerns for my family that were distracting me from the ministry at hand. You've probably experienced those moments when the reality of your life conflicts with what you know is true about God. It's not that you don't believe. You fully believe in God and trust in his love and mercy in your life, but your emotional state is not one of peace and joy. Sometimes, the best prayer most of us can utter at such a time resembles the response of the man whose son was demon possessed. When Jesus asked if he believed, he said honestly, "I believe; help my unbelief!" (Mark 9:24b).

In my struggle, a wonderful pastor friend and his wife encouraged Sara and me by recommending that we listen to a new song by Elevation Worship called "The Blessing." Later that afternoon I downloaded the song, and as the sun set in San Diego, with earphones on, I took in the words and music for the first time. The biblical lyrics, some of which were

151

taken from our scripture for today, were not just true, but compelling and comforting. "The Blessing" continued with passages about how God "... keeps covenant and steadfast love with those who love him and and keep his commandments, to a thousand generations..." (Deuteronomy 7:9). I was absolutely inspired.

But this was only the primer for God's reassuring work in my heart that day. My eyes moistened as I received the blessing of his presence "... going before me, behind me, beside me, all around me, and within me."[1] And as I wept, the following lyrics drove me to my knees:

In the morning, in the evening
In your coming, and your going
In your weeping, and rejoicing
He is for you, He is for you
He is for you, He is for you
He is for you, He is for you
He is for you, He is for you.

I sat on the beach, an emotional jellyfish, and with tears in my eyes I worshiped my God who truly cares for me and blesses me.

As we end our time together in this *on purpose* study, there is nothing better that I could share with you than these words: God is for you! Let me say that again to drive home the reality of this truth: God is for you! He expresses his heart in the blessing that he commanded the high priest Aaron and his sons to pray over the Old Testament people of God. This blessing from Numbers, chapter 6, is not a prayer that Moses wrote. These words did not come from an inspired moment that Aaron had while he was taking a blood sacrifice into the Most Holy Place. These are not wishful words flung into the sky with the hope that somehow we might get God's attention and find his favor. No, this prayer-blessing is nothing less than God's desire for each of us. It is God who commanded the priests to share these words, "Thus you shall bless the people" and "so shall they put my

---

[1] THE BLESSING
Written by Chris Brown, Cody Carnes, Kari Jobe, and Steven Furtick
© 2020 Music by Elevation Worship Publishing (Admin. by Essential Music Publishing LLC) and Remaining portion is unaffiliated

name upon [them]…". If God commands a blessing for his people, he desires it for them and will bring it to fruition in their lives.

My prayer is that thousands of us move forward from this study into a life of following Jesus with this blessing in our minds. Living *on purpose* begins here, right where we are. Here, the God who fully knows who we are (and are not) sends us out with his power and presence and with others whom he has called to do his work. Our "here" is wherever we are reading these words right now. He commands this blessing for our *on purpose* living.

We live *on purpose* with his blessing and within his keeping. His blessing is unmerited favor and goodness upon us, and his keeping is literally his guarding of our lives. The Hebrew words translated here actually refer to building a fence or hedge around a garden. God is for you.

We live *on purpose* as God's face shines upon us. The Israelite rabbis referred to this as the *shekinah*, that indescribable radiance and light that only comes from God. This is similar to "…may the Lord lift up his countenance upon you." It's the Hebrew word *panyim* or "face" that is translated "countenance" here. Even more intimate than what Moses experienced on Mt. Sinai, we now experience God's glory and God's face through the person of Jesus Christ and his Spirit living *in* us. God is for you.

We live *on purpose* by the grace of God. We don't accomplish things in his name because we are super-spiritual men or women. We are not important because we have earned it (we can't), nor are we better than others. We could never find purpose on our own. But through Jesus, God has been gracious to us. It is by the grace of God that we can be used of God. God is for you.

Finally, we live *on purpose* in the peace of God. Most people are restless, wandering or racing through life unable to find meaning and any sense of belonging. But as we follow Jesus and become the people he has made us to be, we find peace. Only in him will we find the soul contentment that is far better than the elusive "happiness" that the world seeks. God is for you.

You are ready to move forward with eternal purpose, but not through your own determination or power. Your purpose comes only through the blessing of God. So read the verses above quietly and slowly once again. And with this blessing, take the first step and then every step as God guides you, and live *on purpose*.

CAN I GO IN PEACE?
EXODUS 4:18-20

Days 36-40

Finally, you and I need to know that what we are doing matters--that there's purpose and meaning in our efforts. We know that God has called every one of us to share our gifts in such a way that those around us see him. Perhaps we need just one final push, one final vote of affirmation, and one final blessing that moves us forward. In this week's study, Moses asks his father-in-law for a blessing to follow God's call. In our hearts, you and I are asking our heavenly father for the same blessing. We want to be certain that God affirms the calling, the gifts, and the purpose he is asking of us.

Let's get started. . .

1. Our Sunday time was powerful. Take a moment and reflect on our worship gathering. What impressions did you have? Also, what encouraged you as you read day the Day Thirty-Six devotional?

2. Watch the video "Can I Go in Peace?" Discuss what you learned and anything that challenged you. Mike encouraged each of us to take a small step of obedience and faith using the following three actions:

   • "Make A Commitment." What are you going to do?

   • "Go All In." What is your next step?

   • "Watch What God Does." How is the Holy Spirit directing you?

154

3. This week's devotionals shared some of the blessings found in scripture designed to encourage us in our journey. Which one meant the most to you?

4. Just as you are called to fulfill a purpose individually, your group is called to do so collectively. Take some time and complete the Small Group Purpose exercise found on page (APPENDIX).

5. As you end your group gathering time, take turns sharing the purpose statement (found on page . . .) that you've created through this study. After everyone has shared, have another group member read out loud Numbers 6:22-27 as a prayer-filled blessing.

Ok, so now what. . .

Final Takeaway. . . What is one specific way you will take your next step toward living on purpose?

_____

_____

_____

Next Steps

- As an individual: Go! Begin living on purpose by taking the next step to use your gifts as God directs.

- As a group: Go! Begin living on purpose. Determine your next gathering time and plan ways to serve those around you.

For Further Reflection

- Study the passages provided in the Week 6 portion of the Appendix.

- Consider what local partnerships and serving opportunities Eastview has for your group to live on purpose

APPENDIX

The following are assessments, resources, and other items that will help you study and evaluate more richly how to live on purpose.

Week 1: Where Am I?

- *Figure Out Your "Here"*

In order to know where to go, we need to know where we've been and where we currently are.

As you evaluate the last 3 months, honestly consider whether you are (circle one):

- running away from Jesus
- wandering aimlessly around
- moving toward Jesus

Now, take a few moments, think back over the last 2 years and answer the following prompts.

Moments:

Name 2 or 3 milestone experiences or moments in the last 2 years that have encouraged you in your Jesus journey.

Motivations:

Who or what keeps you from growing with Jesus?

Who or what helps you keep going with Jesus?

Movements:

What is something Jesus has called you to or might be calling you to do next?

Finally, who are the people and places that God has placed in your life right now that you might be able to influence?

List people (neighbors, friends, family, colleagues, or acquaintances):

List places (neighborhood, school, sports teams, work, or community locations):

1.2 Spiritual Well-Being Assessment (from J.K. Jones)

This assessment takes a snapshot of where you are at in your spiritual journey with Jesus. Take a few minutes, consider the last 2-3 months, and answer authentically. If you do this with the right mindset, you will find your answers to be revealing and freeing. The best results come from the most honest answers. After completing the assessment, prayerfully consider your next steps. We encourage you to share this with those around you and within your small group.

Spiritual Well-Being Assessment (J.K. Jones)

	Very much disagree	Disagree	Neither agree nor disagree	Agree	Very much agree
I am closer to Jesus now than at my conversion.	1	2	3	4	5
I have experienced some personal suffering/pain.	1	2	3	4	5
I have cultivated the organic habit of Word intake that honors God.	1	2	3	4	5
I have cultivated the organic habit of prayer intimacy that honors God.	1	2	3	4	5
I have cultivated the organic habit of worship intensity that honors God.	1	2	3	4	5
I have cultivated the organic habit of community intentionality that honors God.	1	2	3	4	5
I have some unholy habits that burden me.	5	4	3	2	1
I am a good steward of my physical body.	1	2	3	4	5
I believe that I am spiritually healthy.	1	2	3	4	5

Write down any initial thoughts about your results:

What might be one next step that will move you forward in your journey with Jesus?

Week 2: Who Are You, God?

2.1 Further Scripture Study on Who God is

"A simple awareness of God's presence is evidence of his calling us to our purpose. Such awareness can become a holy moment which can in turn heighten our purpose" (A Small Group Ministry Team Member)

Read Exodus 3:14-15 again.

How does God reveal himself?

What do we learn about God's character?

Look up Isaiah 44:6-8, John 1:1-2, and Colossians 1:17. What more do you learn about God?

In discussing how God revealed his name to Moses, John Piper asserts the following:

- "God cannot be stopped from accomplishing his purposes."
- "God does whatever he pleases"
- "God's power is superior to all other powers."

Hold onto these ideas as you read the following. Write down any phrases that help you understand God:

Genesis 1:1

_____

_____

_____

Exodus 15:11 & 26

_____

_____

_____

1 Samuel 2:2

_____

_____

_____

Psalm 86:5-10

_____

_____

_____

Psalm 145

_____

_____

_____

Isaiah 43

_____

_____

_____

Colossians 1:15-20

_____

_____

_____

1 John 1:5

_____

_____

_____

Revelation 1:8

_____

_____

_____

Based upon this week's experience and your study about who God really is, you may want to create some phrases or choose your favorite name for God and create visual reminders. Use your imagination and make signs or pictures and place them around your house, your workplace, or in your car. Let them be an ongoing reminder of God's names and character.

Week 3: Who Am I?

3.1 Who I Am In Christ

The phrases and scripture available below are reminders of who we truly are in Jesus. Often, we lose sight of these truths or begin to believe statements that oppose these promises. Take some time individually and within your group to read each statement out loud. Say each one as loudly and as often as you need to for these truths to take hold of your mind and heart. Once you've gone through this list, take a few moments to highlight, circle, or star the top five phrases that impact you the most.

WHO I AM IN CHRIST?[1]
ORIGINALLY COMPILED BY NEIL ANDERSON

I AM ACCEPTED...	
John 1:21	I am God's child
John 15:15	As a disciple, I am a friend of Jesus Christ
Romans 5:11	I have been justified (declared righteous)
I Corinthians 6:17	I am united with the Lord, and I am one with Him in spirit
I Corinthians 6:9-20	I have been bought with a price and I belong to God
I Corinthians 12:27	I am a member of Christ's body
Ephesians 1:3-8	I have been chosen by God and adopted as His child
Colossians 1:13-14	I have been redeemed and forgiven of all my sins
Colossians 2:9-10	I am complete in Christ

---

[1] *Who Am I In Christ* by Dr. Neil Anderson, Bethany House 2001
https://vintagelawrence.com/wp-content/uploads/2013/01/ANDERSON_WhoIAmInChrist.pdf

| Hebrews 4:14-16 | I have direct access to the throne of grace through Jesus Christ |

I AM SECCURE...

Romans 8:1-2	I am free from condemnation
Romans 8:28	I am assured that God works for my good in all circumstances
Romans 8:31-39	I am free from any condemnation brought against me and I cannot be separated from the love of God
II Corinthians 1:21-22	I have been established, anointed and sealed by God
Colossians 3:1-4	I am hidden with Christ in God
Philippians 1:6	I am confident that God will complete the good work He started in me
Philippians 3:20	I am a citizen of heaven
II Timothy 1:7	I have not been given a spirit of fear but of power, love and a sound mind
I John 5:18	I am born of God and the evil one cannot touch me

I AM SIGNIFICANT...

John 15:5	I am a branch of Jesus Christ, the true vine, and a channel of His life
John 15:16	I have been chosen and appointed to bear fruit
I Corinthians 3:16	I am God's temple
II Corinthians 5:17-21	I am a minister of reconciliation for God
Ephesians 3:12	I may approach God with freedom and confidence
Philippians 4:13	I can do all things through Christ, who strengthens me

3.2 Other Biblical Examples

God uses us, flaws and all, to accomplish His purpose. This is how He has worked throughout the Biblical narrative. For further affirmation that God can, does, and will use all of us, take some time to study the flaws of other biblical men and women. Note and appreciate how God still used them and believe that he will use you, too.

Abraham and Sara - Genesis 17:6,8,15-16

The Prophet Elijah – 1 Kings 17, 18, 19

King David - 1 Samuel 16:11-13

The Messiah - Mark 6:3, John 1:46, John 7:15

Peter - Matthew 4:18, Acts 4:13

Paul - Acts 8:3

What other stories from Scripture come to mind where God took the weaknesses of individuals and used them for his good works?

Consider the following thoughts and quotations:

"God never calls us to any kingdom responsibility we are capable of pulling off on our own." (Jon Bloom, DesiringGod.org)

*"Moses felt fearful and inadequate. Don't we all feel that way sometimes? Yet God asks us to put His purposes for our lives into practice and trust Him with our insecurities." (**A Small Group Ministry Team Member**)*

Why do you think God works this way? Remember that it is "God who works in you." (Philippians 2:12-14)

Week 4: How Can I?

4.1 APEST Spiritual Gift Assessment

Ephesians 4 covers another type of spiritual gifting. This group of gifts is also from the Holy Spirit and it carries the acronym "APEST." Each letter stands for a particular gift that is given by the Holy Spirit within the biblical community of the church.

Apostle Apostles extend the gospel.

Prophet	Prophets know God's will.
Evangelist	Evangelists recruit.
Shepherd	Shepherds nurture and protect with a tender heart.
Teacher	Teachers understand and explain.

If you'd like to learn more about these gifts, we highly encourage you to go to https://5qcentral.com and take the assessment.

Whether you take the spiritual assessment through the church site, or use the APEST assessment, the big question for each of us is:

*"How are you now, or will you in the future, live out
your gifts and calling in your everyday life?"*

4.2 Further Scripture Study

God uses each of us, in our times of struggle, and in our times of success, to accomplish His purposes. As we gain a deeper understanding of, and greater confidence in Jesus, we catch glimpses of his plan. Philip Ryken describes this as "the uncommon faithfulness of common individuals." As you begin to learn about your gifts and how God is calling you to use them, be aware of how you can live on purpose. If God can use a shepherd named Moses with a wooden staff to accomplish all that he did for the nation of Israel, then he can definitely use you.

"God does not call us to a task and then say, 'Have at it.' He equips us for the task. He provides our purpose." (A Small Group Ministry Team Member)

Our purpose is clarified when we experience God's presence, when we are paying attention to Him, and when we ask God, through prayer and scripture, to reveal what He is calling us to do. Spend some time with the following passages and allow them to help you focus on Him.

Psalm 116

_____

_____

_____

John 15:1-5

_____

_____

_____

Ephesians 4

_____

_____

_____

Philippians 4:11-13

_____

_____

_____

Colossians 1:9-13

_____

_____

_____

Week 5: Can You Send Someone Else?

5.1 For Further Scripture Study

Author Paul David Tripp reminds us that we have "God-given gifts and God-given limits." These limits are to remind and encourage us to seek out one another. We discover that we are more complete and more productive if we rely upon God *and* each other. Throughout the Bible, we see God's people being used for different missions and callings. But over and over, through biblical examples, we see that we are not meant to be lone rangers in our gifts and purposes. God has assured us of his presence and of the encouraging presence of fellow believers. Consider the following passages as you prepare to live on purpose:

Joshua 1:7-9

_____

_____

_____

Ephesians 3:14-21

_____

_____

_____

Ephesians 6:10-19

_____

_____

_____

Week 6: Can I Go In Peace?

6.1 Group Purpose Exercise

Small Groups that can clearly articulate their purpose thrive. Use this worksheet to help your group define or redefine its purpose.

4 Purpose Defining Questions

Small groups whose purpose is externally focused exhibit more health, growth and Kingdom impact. As a group answer the following purpose related questions and then define your group's purpose.

GATHER: What compels you and your group to build authentic relationships?

GROW: What are your two next steps in becoming more like Jesus?

GIVE: How can you and your group serve each other and others outside your group?

GO: What people or places can your group specifically influence?

Now, take a shot and define your group's purpose.

Our Group's purpose is . . .

6.2 Further Scripture Study

As you take your next step toward living on purpose, take some time and study the following passages.

Isaiah 26:3-4

_____

_____

_____

John 14:27

_____

_____

_____

Romans 5:1-5

_____

_____

_____

Philippians 4:4-7

_____

_____

_____